TEAM 3 Together

Activity Book

T0386004

Contents

Pearson

New neighbours

1 **Look and match.**

1

2

3

a I'm Lois. I'm eight. I'm British.

b I'm Ash. I'm nine. I'm Australian.

c I'm Lottie. I'm nine. I'm British.

2 **Draw and describe yourself.**

1 What's your name?

_____

2 How old are you?

_____

3 Where are you from?

_____

Countries and nationalities

3 **Look and write the countries.**

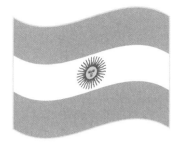

1 C _h i n a_   **2** t _ e U _   **3** A _ g _ _ t _ n _

4 A _ s _ r _ l _ a   **5** T _ _ k _ y   **6** th _ U _ _ _

4 **Look at Activity 3. Read and write the nationalities.**

Turkish   Argentinian   American   Australian   British   ~~Chinese~~

1 My flag is red and yellow.   I'm _____*Chinese*_____ .

2 There are lots of small, white stars on my flag.   I'm _____ .

3 There's a big red cross on my flag.   I'm _____ .

4 My flag is blue with a small red and white cross.   I'm _____ .

5 My flag is white and red.   I'm _____ .

6 My flag is blue and white with a small yellow sun.   I'm _____ .

5 **Write about your flag and your nationality.**

My flag is _____ .

I'm _____ .

1 Complete the crossword.

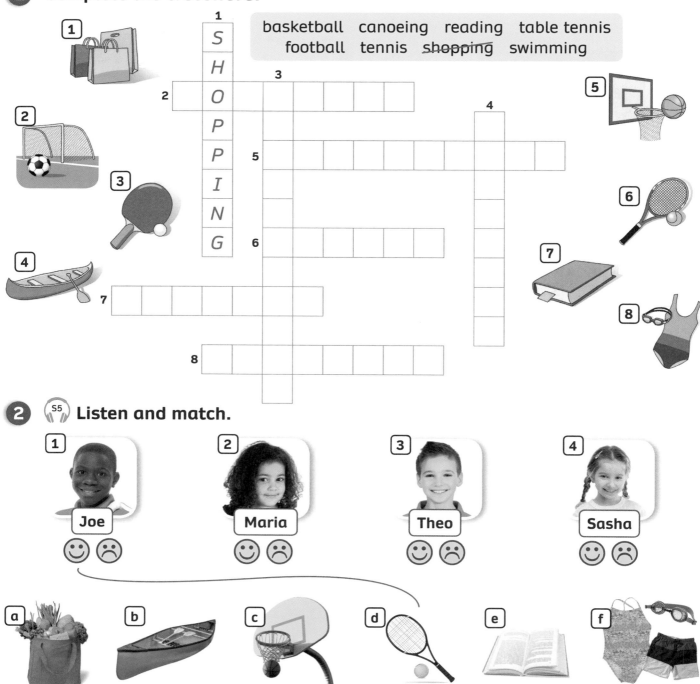

basketball   canoeing   reading   table tennis
football   tennis   ~~shopping~~   swimming

2 (S5) **Listen and match.**

1 Joe ☺ ☹
2 Maria ☺ ☹
3 Theo ☺ ☹
4 Sasha ☺ ☹

a   b   c   d   e   f

3 Look at Activity 2 and complete the sentences. Then write about yourself.

1 Joe likes ___*playing tennis*___. He doesn't like _____.

2 Maria likes _____. She doesn't _____.

3 Theo _____. He _____.

4 Sasha _____. _____.

5 I _____. _____.

1 **Match the numbers.**

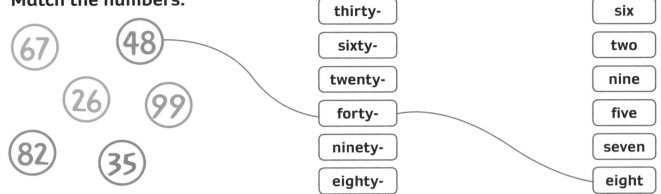

67   48

26   99

82   35

thirty-	six
sixty-	two
twenty-	nine
forty-	five
ninety-	seven
eighty-	eight

2 **Write the missing numbers in words. Then write your own sequence.**

1	thirty	_forty_	fifty	sixty
2	twenty-two	twenty-four	_____	twenty-eight
3	ten	_____	twenty	twenty-five
4	_____	eighty-eight	eighty-seven	eighty-six
5	forty-seven	fifty	_____	fifty-six
6	_____	_____	_____	_____

3 **Write the numbers in words.**

1 45 _forty-five_

2 12 _____

3 29 _____

4 63 _____

5 100 _____

6 77 _____

4 **Follow and solve the riddles. Write the numbers in words.**

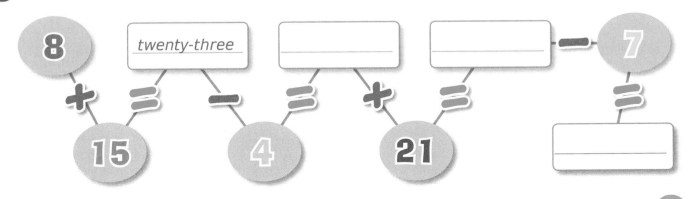

8 + 15 = _twenty-three_ − 4 = _____ + 21 = _____ − 7 = _____

 New school

Vocabulary

1 ⏱ **Look at Pupil's Book page 8 and complete the sentences.**

1 There are children playing _____ and _____.
2 Two girls are _____ on swings and one boy is on a yellow _____.
3 There's a teacher with children in the _____ next to the Maths classroom.

2 **Complete the crossword.**

headteacher

¡Hola!
Spanish

ICT

8−3=5
Maths

PE

Hello!
English

Natural Science

Art

Music   science lab   dinner lady   Social Science

```
 1
 2          H
 3      N   E
 4          A
 5   I      D
 6          T
 7          E
 8          A          C
 9          C
10   P      H
11          E
12          R
```

3 🎯 **Look at Pupil's Book page 8 and write the words.**

1 I can sing and play the piano.   _____Music_____
2 I can play football.   _____
3 I learn about my town.   _____
4 I learn about numbers.   _____
5 I can use a computer.   _____
6 I learn about plants and animals.   _____

I'm learning

Write your crossword definitions to learn new words. Then make a crossword with your words.
I can sing a song. Music.

1 After you read **Look, read and complete.**

Bo   teacher   ICT   ~~Ash~~

First day at a new school!

1 Lottie shows ___Ash___ the school.

2 The _____ introduces Ash to the class.

3 There's a loud noise in the _____ classroom.

4 The children meet _____.

2 **Read the story again. Tick (✓) the rooms which Lottie shows to Ash.**

science lab	✓	Music room	☐
canteen	☐	school office	☐
English classroom	☐	ICT classroom	☐
headteacher's office	☐	Art classroom	☐

3 **Complete the sentences. Can you remember the flag? Where is Ash from?**

Ash is from _____. He's _____.

4 Values **Read and tick (✓). How do you help new friends?**

1 Don't worry! I can show you around. ✓

2 Sorry, I can't help you. I'm reading a book. ☐

3 Who are you? This is not your class. ☐

4 Come and meet my friends Sandy and Ben. ☐

1 🎯 🎧 **1.4 Listen and tick (✓).**

Grammar reference, page 16

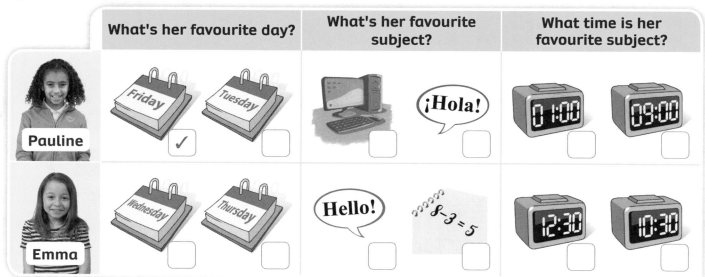

	What's her favourite day?	What's her favourite subject?	What time is her favourite subject?
Pauline	Friday ✓ — Tuesday ☐	computer ☐ — ¡Hola! ☐	01:00 ☐ — 09:00 ☐
Emma	Wednesday ☐ — Thursday ☐	Hello! ☐ — 8–3 = 5 ☐	12:30 ☐ — 10:30 ☐

2 💡 **Look. Is it Pauline's or Emma's timetable?**

	MONDAY	TUESDAY	WEDNESDAY	THURSDAY	FRIDAY
9.00	Maths	Spanish	Maths	English	Maths
10.00			BREAK		
10.30	Social Science	Natural Science	English	Social Science	Natural Science
11.30	English	PE	ICT	Art	PE
12.00			LUNCH		
1.00	Art	ICT	Spanish	ICT	ICT

It's _____ timetable.

3 **Look at the timetable in Activity 2. Answer the questions.**

1 When does she have Spanish? She has Spanish on ___*Tuesday*___ at _____
   and on _____ at _____.

2 What time does she have Art on Thursday? On Thursday, she has Art at _____
   _____.

3 What time does she have lunch every day? She has lunch _____
   _____.

4 When does she have Natural Science? She has _____
   _____.

5 When does she have PE? She _____
   _____.

Vocabulary and Grammar

1 **Find and write the words.**

sometimes always never often

_____	✓✓✓✓✓✓✓
_____	✓✓✓✓✓
sometimes	✓✓✓
_____	✗

2 **Read and match.**

1 three times a week
2 at the weekend
3 every day
4 once a week
5 twice a week

a on Saturday and Sunday
b from Monday to Sunday
c on Wednesday
d on Thursday and Friday
e on Monday, Tuesday and Friday

3 **Look at the diary and complete the sentences with the words from the box.**

always   once a week   sometimes   twice a week   at the weekend

Monday	Tuesday	Wednesday	Thursday	Friday	Saturday	Sunday
lunch school canteen	lunch school canteen	Mum and Dad play tennis	Suzy and I play video games	lunch school canteen	Suzy and I watch TV play video games	Suzy watches TV
listen to music	listen to music	listen to music	listen to music	listen to music	listen to music	listen to music

1 My sister Suzy watches TV _____ _at the weekend_ _____.

2 I _____ listen to music.

3 Mum and Dad play tennis _____.

4 I _____ have lunch in the school canteen.

5 Suzy and I play video games _____.

4 **Write about yourself.**

1 I _____ (always)

2 _____ (often)

3 _____ (at the weekend)

4 _____ (never)

5 _____ (twice a week)

⟫⟫⟫ Extra practice, page 15

CULTURE

1 **Read and complete the puzzles with the words from the box.**

boarding   building   day   Forest   primary   uniform

school

1 Your school now. / The clothes you wear at school.

school

2 You sleep at this school. / It starts at 9 o'clock and finishes at 3 o'clock from Monday to Friday.

school

3 An outdoor lesson. / The place with rooms, doors and windows where you study every day.

2 After you read **Match the sentence halves.**

1 The school day starts at
2 School uniform is often
3 The school day finishes at
4 At a boarding school,
5 A book bag is for
6 Forest School is

a taking books home.
b an outdoor lesson.
c 9 o'clock.
d a jumper, a shirt and a skirt or trousers.
e 3 o'clock.
f children go home at weekends.

3 💬 **Complete. Then compare in pairs.**

My favourite day at school is _____

_____ .

English in action
Making arrangements

1 **Order the words to make sentences.**

Saturday   What   morning   about

[ ]   *What about Saturday morning* _____?

play video games   Do you   tomorrow evening   want to

[1] _____?

at 11 o'clock   Let's   at my house   meet

[ ] _____.

I   Sorry   can't

[ ] _____.

morning   I'm free   Yes   on Saturday

[ ] _____.

2 (1.13) **Order the sentences in Activity 1 to make a dialogue. Then listen and check.**

3 **Plan your weekend. Circle the day. Then ask and answer in pairs and tick (✓) the activities you can do together.**

Activities	When?	Yes (✓)
play tennis	Saturday / Sunday	
go to the park	Saturday / Sunday	
watch a film	Saturday / Sunday	
go to the library	Saturday / Sunday	
go to the supermarket	Saturday / Sunday	
play video games	Saturday / Sunday	

Do you want to play tennis on Saturday?

Sorry, I can't.

Pronunciation

4 (1.14) **Colour the words with the /iː/ sound. Then listen and check.**

feet	peas	kick	knees	men
sleep	fell	bed	clean	swing

Reading

1 **After you read** **Complete the table about Grace's first day at school.**

a quarter to nine   Mr Peers   sandwiches   Art
uniform   Mrs Little   pencil case   walk   Rose

	Grace	You
What to wear to school	1 _uniform_	
School object to take to school	2	
How to get to school	3	
School starts at …	4	
Lunch	5	
Friend	6	
Teacher	7	
Art teacher	8	
Favourite subject	9	

2 **Circle the correct answer.**

1 Grace starts her new school in September / (October).

2 Grace is scared / sad on her first day at school.

3 The school has got a small / great Art room.

4 Grace likes drawing / singing and Art.

5 Grace's picture is on the table / wall of the Art room.

3 **Think about your first day at school and complete the table in Activity 1 for you.**

Writing

1 **Read and underline 13 mistakes. Then write the correct words.**

<u>my</u> brother nick loves school. he studies spanish, english and social science. his favourite subjects are art and natural science. he doesn't like maths.

My _____

_____

2 **Tick (✓) the words which start with a capital letter. Is it the same in your language?**

names	✓	days of the week ☐	subjects ☐
colours	☐	numbers ☐	months ☐

tip **Writing**

Make sure you use a capital letter at the start of each sentence. Use a capital letter for the subject names, too!

3 **Write about your favourite lesson or after-school activity.**

1 Plan

Read and answer. Make notes.

What's your favourite lesson/after-school activity? _____

Why do you like it? _____

What other lesson/activity do you like? _____

Why do you like it? _____

2 Write

Use your notes and write.

My favourite _____

By _____

My favourite _____ is _____.

I like it because _____.

I also like _____. I like it because _____.

3 Check your work ✔

Read your text again and tick (✓).

A capital letter at the start of each sentence? ☐   Correct spelling? ☐   Clear handwriting? ☐

1 Read about Ali's school day. Circle school subjects in red, school places in blue and school jobs in green.

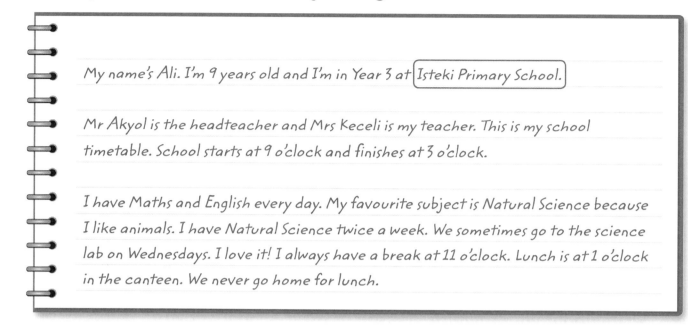

My name's Ali. I'm 9 years old and I'm in Year 3 at Isteki Primary School.

Mr Akyol is the headteacher and Mrs Keceli is my teacher. This is my school timetable. School starts at 9 o'clock and finishes at 3 o'clock.

I have Maths and English every day. My favourite subject is Natural Science because I like animals. I have Natural Science twice a week. We sometimes go to the science lab on Wednesdays. I love it! I always have a break at 11 o'clock. Lunch is at 1 o'clock in the canteen. We never go home for lunch.

2 Write about your school timetable. Then make a presentation for your family.

My name's _____. I'm _____ and I'm in Year
_____ at _____ School.
_____ is the headteacher and _____
my teacher. This is my school timetable. School starts _____
and finishes _____ . My favourite subject _____
because _____ .
I have _____ .
I always have a break _____ . Lunch is _____ .

Self-evaluation

My work in Unit 1 is OK / good / excellent.

My favourite lesson is the one about _____ .

Now I can _____ .

I need to work more on _____ .

1 Find and circle eight school subjects. Then write them in alphabetical order.

N	A	T	U	R	A	L	S	C	I	E	N	C	E
U	X	O	P	M	C	Y	S	V	B	T	U	L	N
G	C	M	D	A	R	T	U	N	D	L	N	V	G
N	E	U	N	T	I	C	S	L	O	I	C	T	L
Y	F	S	F	H	E	H	I	L	F	P	B	X	I
W	N	I	R	S	P	A	N	I	S	H	S	Y	S
S	O	C	I	A	L	S	C	I	E	N	C	E	H
F	E	C	D	E	Z	D	C	C	B	W	Y	R	G

1 ___Art___ 2 _____ 3 _____ 4 _____

5 _____ 6 _____ 7 _____ 8 _____

2 Who works at your school? What do they do?

1 ___Mrs García___ is ___the Maths teacher___ .

2 _____ is _____ .

3 _____ is _____ .

4 _____ is _____ .

3 Look and write sentences.

  has Tuesday  has  twice a week

1 Carmen _____ . 2 Mo _____ .

 sometimes plays  Sundays reads Saturdays

3 Renata _____ . 4 Eduardo _____ .

Vocabulary and Grammar reference

Vocabulary

1 Translate the words into your language. Add more words to the list.

School subjects

Art _____

English _____

ICT _____

Maths _____

Music _____

Natural Science _____

PE _____

Social Science _____

Spanish _____

_____ _____

_____ _____

People at school

dinner lady _____

headteacher _____

_____ _____

_____ _____

Places at school

science lab _____

_____ _____

_____ _____

Frequency adverbs

always _____

often _____

sometimes _____

never _____

_____ _____

every day _____

at the weekend _____

once a week _____

twice a week _____

three times a week _____

Grammar

2 Read and complete.

often   ~~on~~   every   at   has   twice   weekend

Present simple with dates and times				
I/You	have Maths	[1] _on_ Mondays.		
He/She/It	[2] _____ lunch		[3] _____ 1 o'clock.	
We/You/They	don't have Art	at the [4] _____	at half past ten.	

Adverbs of frequency 1		
I/You	always	fly a kite.
He/She/It	[5] _____	plays the guitar.
We/You/They	sometimes never	play tennis.

Adverbs of frequency 2		
I/You	fly a kite	[6] _____ day.
He/She/It	plays the guitar	once a week.
We/You/They	play tennis	[7] _____ a week. three times a week.

Get ready for...

A1 Movers Reading and Writing Part 4

 1 Read the text. Choose the right words and write them on the lines.

My first day at school

My name's Hana. Today is my first day at school. I get up at 8 o'clock **(1)** _every day_ .
Then I have breakfast and I go to school.

The school day **(2)** _____ at 9 o'clock and finishes **(3)** _____
3 o'clock.

My favourite subject is Natural Science. We have it **(4)** _____ a week:
on Monday, Wednesday and Friday.

(5) _____ Fridays we sometimes go to the science lab. I like it because we
learn about plants and animals. I also like PE very much. I **(6)** _____ play
tennis at the weekend: on Saturdays with my parents and on Sundays with my friends.
It's fun!

1 always / every day / morning
2 starts / start / starting
3 in / at / on
4 twice / three times / three
5 At / In / On
6 never / every day / always

Picnic time!

Vocabulary

1 🕐 **Look at Pupil's Book page 20 and complete the sentences.**

1 There are lots of children playing _____.

2 The _____ flag is blue, white and yellow.

3 The baby wants to have a _____. The boy is hungry because he wants to have some _____.

2 **Find and number.**

cupcakes ☐   tea ☐

salad ☐   lemonade ☐ *1*

sandwiches ☐   noodles ☐

coffee ☐   milkshake ☐

fruit ☐   crisps ☐

cereal ☐   vegetables ☐

3 **Look at Activity 2 and complete the table.**

sweet	savoury	other
cupcakes		

I'm learning

Draw pictures of new words to help you remember them. Make your own flashcards.

4 💡 **Can you think of another category to classify food? Write some examples.**

1 After you read Look, read and order.

Lemonade comes from lemons!

The Secret Shed

Noodles and lemonade! Yum!

`1`

I know! We can have our Discovery Team meetings here!

Let's form the Discovery Team!

Bo learns a lot of new things every day.

2 🔍 **Write all the food and drink words you see in Activity 1.**

noodles _____ _____ _____ _____

3 Complete the sentences.

1 The children have a _____*picnic*_____ in Ash's garden.
2 Bo wants to put _____ on _____.
3 The children form a _____.
4 The children have their team's meetings in an old _____.
5 The children find the club symbol on the _____.

4 ✓ Values **Read and circle.**

The story is about learning together / doing exercise / working hard.

1 🎧 2.5 **Listen and tick (✓).**

Grammar reference, page 28

1
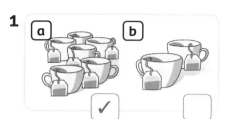

2

3
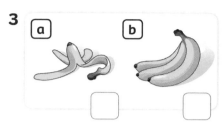

4
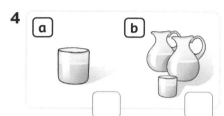

5

6
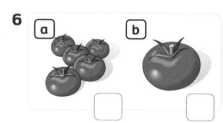

2 **Look at the pictures *a* in Activity 1. Then complete the sentences.**

a lot of   are   little   isn't   a few   any

1 There's _____*a lot of*_____ tea.
2 There are _____ apples.
3 There aren't _____ bananas.
4 There's a _____ lemonade.
5 There _____ any bread.
6 There _____ a lot of tomatoes.

3 💥 **What's on your plate?**
Draw and write.

On my plate, _there's a little bread._

_____
_____
_____
_____
_____

4 💬 **Compare with your partner. Are your plates the same or different?**

On my plate, there's a tomato.

On my plate, there aren't any tomatoes.

Vocabulary and Grammar

1 **Look at the pictures. Find the containers and complete the phrases.**

B	I	D	R	I	N	B	O	W	L
O	K	P	L	A	T	E	F	B	I
T	V	E	G	C	L	A	S	A	S
T	E	S	O	A	F	W	A	G	T
L	E	R	E	N	V	E	B	O	X
E	R	Y	D	A	Y	A	N	D	Y
C	U	P	O	G	L	A	S	S	U

1 **1** a _____*can*_____ of lemonade

2 **2** a _____ of water

3 **3** a _____ of salad

4 **4** a _____ of tea

5 **5** a _____ of orange juice

6 **6** a _____ of cupcakes

7 **7** a _____ of eggs

8 **8** a _____ of carrots

💡 What's the message? *I drink ...* _____

2 (2.10) **Write questions with *any*. Then listen and circle.**

1	fruit	*Is there any fruit?*	Yes/No
2	apples		Yes /No
3	oranges		Yes /No
4	orange juice		Yes /No
5	bananas		Yes /No
6	ice cream		Yes /No

3 💬 **Look at Activity 2. In pairs, ask and answer.**

> Is there any fruit?   Yes, there is.

CULTURE

1 **Look and match. Then say.**

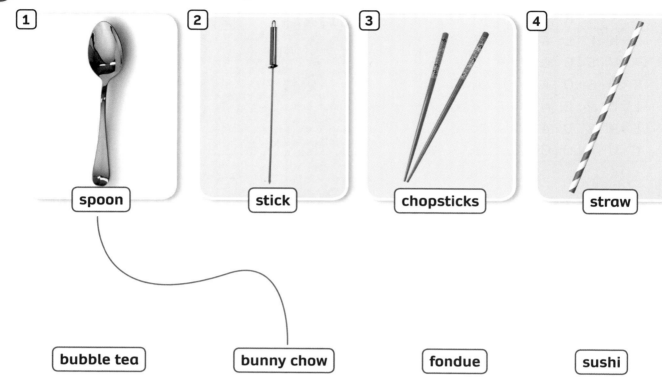

1 spoon

2 stick

3 chopsticks

4 straw

bubble tea

bunny chow

fondue

sushi

2 **After you read** **Read and write _True_ or _False_.**

1 You eat bunny chow with chopsticks. _____False_____

2 Bubble tea is popular in Asia. _____

3 Fondue can be sweet or savoury. _____

4 You make sushi with noodles. _____

5 You make bunny chow with cake. _____

3 **Correct the false sentences in Activity 2.**

_____

_____

_____

_____

_____

English in action
Shopping for food

1 🎯 **Read and choose the best answer.**

1 Can I help you?
   (a) Hello. Can I have some apples, please?
   b Anything else?
   c Here you are.

2 Can I have four cupcakes, please?
   a No, thanks.
   b Here you are.
   c No, that's it.

3 Anything else?
   a Thanks, bye.
   b That's four pounds, please.
   c No, that's it, thanks.

4 That's one pound, please.
   a Hello, can I help you?
   b Here you are.
   c Anything else?

2 **Order the sentences to make a dialogue.**

[ ] No, that's it.

[**1**] Good morning! Can I help you?

[ ] Right. That's two pounds, please.

[ ] Here you are.

[ ] Hi! Can I have three bags of grapes, please?

[ ] Thanks! Bye.

[ ] One, two, three. Anything else?

Pronunciation

3 🎧 (2.15) **Colour the words with the /aɪ/ sound. Then listen and check.**

white	juice	eye	dinner	rice
fly	**tea**	**right**	**say**	**pair**

Reading

1 `After you read` **Read and circle.**

1 Dora Patterson is the winner of the TV show
Little Chef / (Kids Cook)!

2 Dora lives in Oxford / London.

3 Dora has got one dog / cat.

4 Welsh rarebit is Dora's / Baxter's favourite recipe.

5 Welsh rarebit is cereal / cheese on toast / eggs.

2 **Circle the words and complete the ingredients.**

(minutes) breadsalteggpeoplemilkcheese

Welsh rarebit   🕐 Time: 10 _minutes_   👥 For: 4 _____

Ingredients:

1 _____   2 _____   3 _____   4 _____   5 _____

3 **Read and correct the mistakes.**

mix ~~bread~~ mixture bowl grill

Welsh rarebit

1 You toast some <u>cheese</u>.   _bread_

2 You put the cheese, yolk, milk and salt into a <u>box</u>.   _____

3 You <u>toast</u> the ingredients together.   _____

4 You put the <u>ingredients</u> on the bread.   _____

5 You put the bread with the mixture under the <u>fish</u>. _____

Writing

tip Writing
When you explain how to do something, use these words: *first, then, after that* and *last.*

1 Order the steps of the recipe. Then complete.

After ~~First~~ Last Then

Tomato noodles

☐ _____ that, you take the noodles out of the water.

1 ___First___ , you put the noodles in hot water and cook for four minutes.

☐ _____ , you put the tomatoes on the noodles.

☐ _____ , you put the tomatoes in the oil.

2 Plan and write a recipe.

1 Plan

Read and answer. Make notes.

- What's the name of your food? _____
- What ingredients do you need? _____
- How long does it take to make? _____
- How many people is it for? _____
- How do you make it? _____

2 Write

Use your notes and write.

My favourite recipe!

_____

Time: _____   For: _____

INGREDIENTS: _____

_____

INSTRUCTIONS:

- First, you _____.
- Then, you _____.
- After that, you _____.
- Last, you _____.

3 Check your work ✓

Read your text again and tick (✓).

List of ingredients? ☐   Correct spelling? ☐   Clear handwriting? ☐

1 💡 **It's your birthday. Choose your birthday party menu! Decide what food and drink there is or isn't at your party. Then complete the table.**

crisps   cupcakes   cans of lemonade   sandwiches   ~~burgers~~   rice
fruit   vegetables   salad   bowls of ice cream   bread   noodles   sweets
bottles of milk   glasses of water   cheese   pasta   eggs

a lot of	some	a few	a little	no
burgers				

2 **Look at Activity 1 and write about your birthday party menu. Draw a picture.**

Happy Birthday!

At my party there _are a lot of burgers._

_____

_____

_____

_____

_____

_____

3 💬 **Compare your birthday party menus in pairs.**

> Are there any burgers at your birthday party?

> Yes, there are a lot of burgers!

Self-evaluation

My work in Unit 2 is OK / good / excellent.

My favourite lesson is the one about _____.

Now I can _____.

I need to work more on _____.

Extra practice

1 Match the words to make six types of food and drink.

vege

cup

cake

lemon

sand

wich

real

les

ce

nood

tables

ade

2 Circle the correct answer.

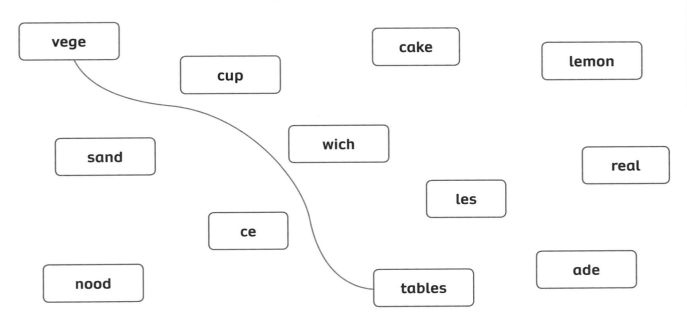

1 There are /(is) a lot of bread.
2 There isn't / aren't any lemonade.
3 There are some crisps / coffee.
4 There are a few salad / apples.

3 Circle eight containers in the wordsnake.

secanpiplatemstboxakwbottleyesglassastbagvgcupkibowlng

4 Complete the questions. Then answer them. Use short answers.

1 Are there any tomatoes? ✓ _Yes, there are._
2 Is there any milk? ✗ _____
3 _____ any cheese? ✓ _____
4 _____ bananas? ✓ _____
5 _____ tea? ✗ _____

Vocabulary and Grammar reference

Vocabulary

1 **Translate the words into your language. Add more words to the list.**

Food

cereal _____

coffee _____

crisps _____

cupcakes _____

fruit _____

milkshake _____

lemonade _____

noodles _____

salad _____

sandwiches _____

tea _____

vegetables _____

_____ _____

_____ _____

_____ _____

Containers

a bag _____

a bottle _____

a bowl _____

a box _____

a can _____

a cup _____

a glass _____

a plate _____

_____ _____

_____ _____

_____ _____

_____ _____

Grammar

2 **Read and complete.**

> a few   a little   sandwiches   aren't
> water   's   ~~are~~   any

Countable		
There ¹ _are_	a lot of some ² _____	³ _____ cans of lemonade. apples.
There ⁴ _____	any	cupcakes.

Uncountable		
There ⁵ _____	a lot of some ⁶ _____	salad. ⁷ _____ coffee.
There isn't	⁸ _____	cheese.

A1 Movers Listening Part 1

Do! **1** 🎯 🎧 2.18 **Listen and draw lines.**

Jack   Sam   Lisa

Anna   David   Tina

3 Along the river

Vocabulary

1 ⏱ **Look at Pupil's Book page 32 and complete the sentences.**

1 Lois has got a _____bottle of water_____ in one hand and an _____ in the other.

2 She has got a _____ with a cupcake on it, too.

3 In one poster, there's a _____ river. In the other poster, there's a small _____on the lake.

2 **Look and find. Then complete the missing letters.**

| 1 | 2 | 3 | 4 | 5 | 6 | 7 | 8 | 9 |

| ll | and | ke | est | fall | er | tain | wn | ty |

isl _and_   for____   riv____   water____   to____   hi____   la____   moun___   ci____

3 **Look and complete.**

high   wide   deep

The lake is _____.   The river is _____.   The mountain is _____.

I'm learning

Play spelling games to remember new words and practise spelling: I-S-L-A-N-D.

1 **After you read** **What's the problem?**
Look, read and match.

The Great Clean-up

1

2

3

4 · a

a   The bags are too big for Lottie.
b   Bo can't put the gloves on.
c   The forest is beautiful, but the river is very dirty.
d   Ash and Bo can't put the wood in the bag.

2 🔍 **Look at Activity 1 and find two landscape words.**

_____   _____

3 **Answer the questions.**

1   Why are the children in the forest?

Because it's The Great Clean-up.

2   What do the children wear to pick up the rubbish?

_____

3   What rubbish do the children find?

_____

4   What can the children do with all that rubbish?

_____
_____

4 ⭐ **Values** **Read and tick (✓). How do you look after nature?**
Add one more idea.

1   Let's throw the rubbish in the river. ☐

2   Let's help to clean the forest at a clean-up. ✓

3   Let's use old cans and bottles to make new decorations. ☐

4   Let's throw the rubbish in the bin. ☐

5   _____

1 Complete the sentences. Then circle *True* or *False*.

Grammar reference, page 40

1 Salt is _____*sweeter*_____ (sweet) than sugar. True / (False)

2 Mexico is _____ (cold) than Antarctica. True / False

3 Beijing is _____ (big) than London. True / False

4 Trains are _____ (old) than planes. True / False

5 Fingers are _____ (short) than toes. True / False

6 Trousers are _____ (long) than shorts. True / False

2 3.5 Listen and match.

| Ian | Mark | Abby | Sophie | Mia |

3 Look at Activity 2 and complete the sentences.

~~happy~~   angry   sad   tall   dirty

1 Mia is _____*the happiest*_____ of all.

2 Mark is _____ of all.

3 Sophie is _____ of all.

4 Ian _____ of all.

5 Abby _____ .

1 **Read and write the words.**

exciting   <u>interesting</u>   delicious   beautiful   boring   famous   dangerous   difficult

1 This TV programme is

_____<u>interesting</u>_____ .

2 This singer is

_____.

3 This salad is

_____.

4 This book is

_____.

5 This lake is

_____.

6 This animal is

_____.

7 This problem is

_____.

8 This activity is

_____.

2 **Look and complete the sentences.**

	delicious	big	dangerous	dirty	boring
●	apples	cats	lake	the bathroom	Art
●●	oranges	tigers	river	the kitchen	Maths
●●●	bananas	elephants	waterfall	my bedroom	Social Science

1 Oranges are _<u>more delicious</u>_ than apples, but bananas are the _<u>most delicious</u>_ .

2 Tigers are _____ than cats, but elephants are the _____.

3 This river is _____ than this lake, but this waterfall is the _____.

4 My bedroom is the _____ room in our house.

5 I think that Social Science is _____ than Art and Maths.

3 💬 **Answer the questions. Then compare your answers in pairs.**

1 Who is the tallest person in your family? _____

2 What is more dangerous, a tiger or a crocodile? _____

3 What is more difficult, Maths or English? _____

4 Which is the most boring programme on TV? _____

5 What is more delicious, a cupcake or an ice cream? _____

» Extra practice, page 39

CULTURE

1 **Look and write.**

bear   alligator   panther   ~~wolf~~   turtle

1   2   3   4   5

wolf

2 **What's the animal? Read and write.**

turtle   alligator   ~~bear~~   panther   wolf

1   I'm big and my fur is brown. I sleep a lot in winter.   _bear_

2   I've got a big shell and I can swim.

3   I like meat and I live in a group.

4   I'm black and I've got a long tail.

5   I've got sharp teeth and a long tail. I live in rivers and lakes.

3   After you read   **Choose the correct answer.**

1   There are more than 58 (national parks)/ parks in the USA.

2   The Grand Canyon National Park is
    in Florida / Arizona.

3   The Grand Canyon is over a kilometre /
    three kilometres deep.

4   In Yellowstone National Park you can
    see the deepest / highest lake in the USA.

5   There are bears / alligators in Yellowstone
    National Park.

6   You can take boat / bike trips to see birds
    in the Everglades National Park.

English in action 3
Asking the way

1 **Reorder the letters.**

1 Turn *left*.
(ftel)

2 Turn
_____ .
(grtih)

3 Go
_____ _____
ahead.
(isrttahg)

4 Go
_____ _____
the road.
(rascso)

5 Go _____
the shop to
the park.
(mfor)

6 Go _____
the road.
(glnao)

2 (3.15) **Listen and write. Then draw on the map.**

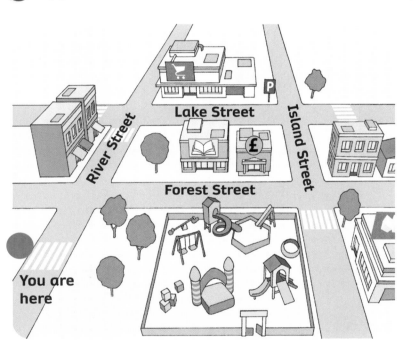

Lake Street
River Street
Island Street
Forest Street
£

You are here

> Excuse me, can you tell me the way to the Ice Supermarket, please?

> Sure. Go ___*across*___ River Street and turn _____.
> Then turn right into _____ Street and go straight _____. Next turn right _____ the playground and go across Island Street. The Ice Supermarket is on your _____.

> OK. Thank you!

Pronunciation

3 (3.16) **Colour the words with the /eɪ/ sound. Then listen and check.**

take	**right**	**kite**	**play**	**grey**
dance	**day**	**ice**	**wait**	**key**

Reading

---

1 `After you read` **Look and read. Circle the odd one out.**

1

a white water
b (glass of water)
c river

2

a tired
b can't swim
c can't move

3

a emergency signal
b loud sound
c song

4

a city
b hills
c mountains

5

a London
b Arizona
c Phoenix

2 **Read and write *True* or *False*.**

1 Luke lives in Arizona, USA.   *True*
2 The most important river in Arizona is
   the Colorado River.   _____
3 Jake and Luke go hiking in the Grand Canyon.   _____
4 Luke's leg is hurt.   _____
5 Jake blows a whistle six times.   _____
6 The helicopter takes Luke home.   _____

3 **Correct the false sentences in Activity 2.**

Jake and Luke go canoeing in the Grand Canyon.
_____

_____

3

Writing

tip Writing

Remember to use capital letters for names of places: Santa Cruz, San Lorenzo, Deseado River, Los Glaciares National Park

1 **Correct the mistakes and rewrite the text. Then write about you.**

this is amrita, she lives at 113 karnataka road, bangalore, india. and you? where do you live?

This is Amrita. _____

_____

| About you | I'm _____. I live at _____
_____. |

2 **Write a fact file about your region.**

1 Plan

Read and answer. Make notes.

What's the capital city? _____

What's the landscape like? _____

What's the highest mountain/longest river/biggest lake? _____

What's your favourite place? _____

2 Write

Use your notes and write. Then draw.

Fact File

Capital city: _____

_____

_____

_____

_____

3 Check your work ✔

Read your fact file again and tick (✓).

A capital letter for all names of places? ☐   Correct spelling? ☐   Clear handwriting? ☐

1   **Look at the map. Read and choose.**

Barnfield National Park

This is Barnfield National Park. There's a short and a long walk to get to the Old Castle. The Blue Walk is *longer* / (*shorter*) and more interesting. On the Blue walk, there are *two* / *three* mountains and two *lakes* / *rivers*. There's also a beautiful forest and *a waterfall* / *an island*. It's the highest waterfall in the national park.

From the Brown Shed to the Old Castle on the Blue Walk
Go straight ahead. Turn *right* / *left* at the mountain. Go *straight ahead* / *across* and turn right at the waterfall. Go along the two *waterfalls* / *rivers* and turn right at the mountain. Go *left* / *across* the forest and the Old Castle is on the right.

2   **Look at the map again. Write about the Red walk.**

~~long~~   exciting   deep   beautiful   big

The Red Walk   *is longer than the Blue Walk*   .

There are _____

_____ .

There's a _____

_____ .

3   **Give directions from the Brown Shed to the Old Castle on the Red Walk.**

Go _____ . Turn _____ .

Go _____

_____ .

Self-evaluation

My work in Unit 3 is OK / good / excellent.

My favourite lesson is the one about _____ .

Now I can talk _____ .

I need to work more on _____ .

1 **Find and write.**

1

forest

2

3

4

forest waterfall lake hill city island town river mountain

5

6

7

8

9

2 **Look at the differences and write.**

beautiful ~~high~~ dirty small wide delicious

a

b

c

1 (mountain) *The mountain in picture c is higher than the mountain in picture b, but the mountain in picture a is the highest.*

2 (river) _____

3 (forest) _____

4 (tent) _____

5 (bird) _____

6 (food) _____

Vocabulary and Grammar reference

Vocabulary

1 **Translate the words into your language. Add more words to the list.**

Landscape		Adjectives	
city	_____	deep	
forest	_____	high	_____
hill	_____	wide	_____
island	_____	_____	_____
lake	_____		
mountain	_____	beautiful	_____
river	_____	boring	_____
town	_____	dangerous	_____
waterfall	_____	delicious	_____
_____	_____	difficult	_____
_____	_____	exciting	_____
		famous	_____
		interesting	_____
		_____	_____
		_____	_____

Grammar

2 **Read and complete.**

biggest   more   bigger   most   ~~than~~

Comparative adjectives (short)		
This mountain is	higher [1] _____than_____	that hill.
Buenos Aires is	[2] _____ than	London.
Comparative adjectives (long)		
This lake is	more beautiful than	that river.
Canoeing is	[3] _____ exciting than	swimming.

Superlative adjectives (short)		
Mount Everest is	the highest	mountain in the world.
London is	the [4] _____ city	in the UK.
Superlative adjectives (long)		
Chocolate cupcakes are	the [5] _____ delicious	cupcakes of all.
Canoeing is	the most exciting	sport of all.

Get ready for...

A1 Movers Listening Part 5

Do! **1** **3.20** **Listen and colour and write.**

Language booster 1

1 **Read and circle.**

1 The salad is on the (top) / bottom shelf.

2 The lemonade is above / below the salad.

3 The vegetables are on the top / bottom shelf.

4 The cupcakes are above / below the vegetables.

5 Look up / down at the eggs.

6 Look up / down at the sandwiches.

2 **Choose and write.**

below   Brilliant   down   top   ~~where~~

Excuse me, ¹ ___where___ are the cupcakes?

They're on the ² _____ shelf.

And where are the sandwiches?

Look ³ _____ . They're on the bottom shelf, ⁴ _____ the eggs.

⁵ _____ ! Thanks.

3 **Look at Activity 1 and complete the sentences.**

1 The chocolate is _____ shelf.

2 The eggs _____ the sandwiches.

3 The lemonade is _____ shelf.

4 The vegetables _____ the cupcakes.

4 **Match the questions and answers.**

1 Where are you?

2 Who are you with?

3 What are you doing?

4 Why are you buying cupcakes?

5 When is the party?

a We're buying cupcakes.

b For my birthday party.

c I'm at the supermarket.

d Tomorrow at two o'clock.

e I'm with my mum.

5 **Find the question words and complete the sentences.**

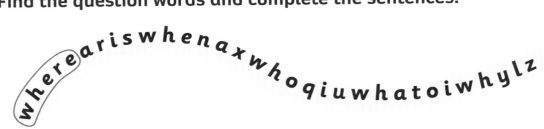

whereariswhenaxwhoqiuwhatoiwhylz

1 _____ is your favourite singer?

2 _____Where_____ do you go after school?

3 _____ do you like holidays?

4 _____ is your favourite food?

5 _____ is your birthday?

6 **Look at Activity 5. Answer the questions and draw.**

1 _____

2 _____

3 _____

4 _____

5 _____

I like holidays because I go to the beach.

All about jobs

Vocabulary

1 ⏱ **Look at Pupil's Book page 48 and complete the sentences.**

1   On the table, I can see a ____plate____ of sandwiches and three _____ of water.

2   There's a book about _____ next to the English book.

3   Lois is laughing because Ash is a _____ in the game.

2 **Look and write.**

> musician   scientist   singer   farmer   headteacher   vet   firefighter   chef
> police officer   bus driver   actor/actress   mechanic   waiter/waitress

_____

_____

3 **Look at Activity 2. What's the extra word?**

The extra word is _____.

I'm learning

Make job wheels to help you remember new words.
Think of more ideas.

1 **After you read** **Look, read and match. Then circle. Who says what?**

1	There's a car outside Ash's house.	(Lois)/ Lottie / Ash / Bo
	That isn't a burglar! That's Alesha!	Lois / Lottie / Ash / Bo
	He's upstairs!	Lois / Lottie / Ash / Bo
	He's wearing jeans and a yellow jacket.	Lois / Lottie / Ash / Bo

2 **Tick the jobs you can see in Picture 1 of the story.**

✓ vet   ☐ mechanic   ☐ musician   ☐ singer   ☐ waitress

☐ actor   ☐ actress   ☐ firefighter   ☐ bus driver   ☐ police officer

3 **Circle the correct word.**

1 Ash is visiting (friends)/family today.

2 Bo is playing a vet / mechanic.

3 The 'burglar' is drinking some milk / water.

4 The 'burglar' is a boy / girl.

5 The 'burglar' is Alex / Alesha.

6 Alesha is Ash's cousin / friend.

4 **Values** **What do you think? Read and circle.**

The story is about taking care of your parent's car / books / friends and neighbours.

Grammar

1 🎯 🎧 (4.5) **What are they doing on Activity Day? Listen and write a letter.**

Grammar reference, page 54

a

b

Tracy ☐

Daniel b

c

d

David and Emilia ☐

Chloe ☐

e

f

2 **Look at Activity 1 and complete the questions and answers.**

1 ___Is___ Daniel making sandwiches?   ___No___, he ___isn't___.

2 _____ David playing football?   _____, _____.

3 _____ David and Emilia playing tennis?   _____, they _____.

4 _____ Chloe having cupcakes for lunch?   _____, she _____.

5 _____ Tracy taking photos of the kites?   _____, she _____.

3 **Look at Activity 1 and 2 again. Then write.**

1 Daniel isn't ___making sandwiches___. He's making ___cupcakes___.

2 David isn't _____. He's _____.

3 David and Emilia are _____.

4 Chloe isn't _____. She's _____.

5 Tracy _____.

4 💬 **In pairs, mime an action and guess.**

Look! What am I doing?

You're playing tennis.

Vocabulary and Grammar

1 Look and complete.

be break be quiet follow put arrive drop shout

1

_____be_____ late

2

_____ in class

3

_____ the rules

4

_____ on time

5

_____ litter in the bin

6

_____ in class

7

_____ litter

8

_____ the rules

2 🎯 Read the song again and choose.

You **(1)**___must___ buy your ticket
and you **(2)**_____ drop any litter!

You must **(3)**_____ your litter in the
bin and **(4)**_____ the rules when
you're playing here!

You **(5)**_____, you mustn't be late
when you come to eat every day!

Quiet, please! You **(6)**_____be quiet
when you're learning Science.

1 aren't must doesn't	**4** following follow follows
2 must doesn't mustn't	**5** must shout shout mustn't shout
3 put putting puts	**6** mustn't must doesn't

3 ✳ Write one rule with *must* and one with *mustn't*. Draw the signs. In pairs, compare and say all the rules.

do your homework   help at home
go to bed late   tidy up your room
eat a lot of fruit   eat a lot of sweets

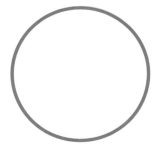 

_____

_____

⟫⟫ Extra practice, page 53

CULTURE

1 **Match the jobs with the pictures.**

1	The Queen's Piper
2	A professional tea taster
3	The Raven Master

a ☐

raven

b ☐

cups of tea

c ☐

black and red uniform

d ☐

long spoon

e 1

bagpipes

f ☐

kilt

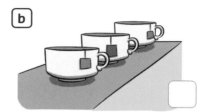

2 **After you read** **Complete the sentences.**

300   6   15   9   ~~5~~

1 You must train for ___5___ years to be a professional tea taster.

2 The Tower of London has _____ ravens.

3 The Queen's piper plays for Her Majesty for about _____ minutes.

4 Professional tea tasters try _____ cups of tea every day.

5 The Queen's Piper plays the bagpipes at _____ am.

3 ✳ **Imagine you do one of the jobs in Activity 1. Write about your job. Then tell your class.**

I'm a _____ .

I must _____ .

I wear _____ .

I like my job because _____ .

English in action (4)
Calling the emergency services

1 💡 **When must you make an emergency call? Read and tick.**

- ✓ there's a fire in the science lab
- ☐ my homework is at the park
- ☐ my sister can't move
- ☐ I can't find my school bag

- ☐ my granny's leg is hurt
- ☐ my cat isn't eating
- ☐ I'm angry
- ☐ there's a burglar in my neighbour's house

2 🎧(4.14) **Listen and complete for Tom.**

		Tom	You
1	What service do you need?	*an ambulance*	
2	What's your name?	Tom _____	
3	What's your address?	_____ Park _____	
4	What's your phone number?	77 _____	
5	What's the emergency?	My sister's got a _____	

3 💬 **Think about an emergency and complete the *You* column in Activity 2. In pairs, practise the emergency call.**

Pronunciation

4 🎧(4.15) **Colour the words with the /ŋ/ sound at the end. Then listen and check.**

breaking	dancing	legs	skipping	bend
chicken	feeding	plane	penguin	calling

Reading

1 **After you read** What's their job? Follow the lines and write.

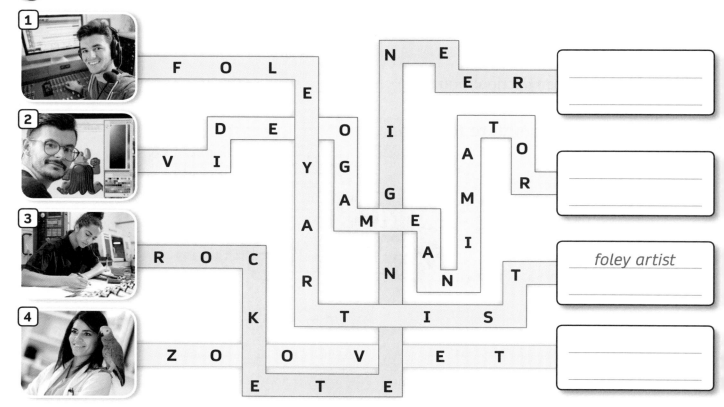

1 _____

2 _____

3 *foley artist*
_____

4 _____

2 Answer the questions.

1 How many different jobs are there in the text?

There are four jobs.

2 What must a video game animator do before he or she animates a person in a game?

_____

3 What kind of animals does a zoo vet take care of?

_____

4 How can you make the sound of a bird's wings?

_____

5 What does a rocket engineer look at before he or she puts the rocket together?

_____

3 ✴ Imagine you're a video game animator. Draw a new game character. Then show it to the class.

Writing

1 **Write about your survey and what you want to be when you grow up.**

1 Plan

In groups, make a survey. Ask the questions and complete the table.

Name	Job	Why?
Abdul	zoo vet	love zoos and animals

What do you want to be when you grow up?

I want to be a zoo vet.

Why?

Because I love zoos and animals.

2 Write

Use the information in Activity 1. Draw a graph and write.

Jobs report

By _____

Here are my results.

_____ wants to be _____ because

_____

and _____ wants to be _____

because _____

_____ .

When I grow up, I want to be _____

because _____ .

tip Writing

We use a new paragraph to show a new idea.

3 Check your work ✓

Read your fact file again and tick (✓).

A paragraph for each idea? ☐   Correct spelling? ☐   Clear handwriting? ☐

1 **Read and circle the jobs. Then underline the rules.**

Today it's Jobs Day at our school. It's a lot of fun! You must wear a job uniform and you mustn't be late!

Years 1 and 2 are working as vets. They are looking after their teddy bears. They must wash them but they mustn't feed them! Years 3 and 4 are working in a restaurant. Year 3 want to eat something. They must buy food and drinks. Year 4 are the

chefs, waiters and waitresses. The chefs are cooking lunch and the waiters and waitresses are laying the tables. They must clean the tables and put any litter in the bin.

Years 5 and 6 are working as firefighters and police officers. There's an emergency at school! They must wear their uniforms. Everybody must follow their rules.

2 **Imagine it's Jobs Day at your school. Write.**

Today it's Jobs Day at our school. It's a lot of fun!

You must _____.

You mustn't _____.

Years 1 and 2 _____

_____.

Years 3 and 4 _____

_____.

Years 5 and 6 _____

_____.

Self-evaluation

My work in Unit 4 is OK / good / excellent.

My favourite lesson is the one about _____.

Now I can _____.

I need to work more on _____.

1 💡 **Read the riddles and write the jobs. There are four extra words.**

scientist   ~~farmer~~   chef   bus driver   firefighter   vet   waiter   actress

1 I work with animals but I'm not a doctor.
I feed them and they feed me!
Milk, cheese and eggs,
And a scarf for winter days!
farmer

2 You can see me in the theatre,
You can see me on TV,
You can see me singing and dancing,
In many beautiful films.

3 I work in a beautiful restaurant,
Called 'The Hungry Elephant',
What do I do?
I cook delicious food for you!

4 I don't drive a police car,
I don't drive a train,
But if you buy a ticket,
I can take you to a park.

2 💥 **Write a riddle for one of the extra words in Activity 1.**

3 **Order the words to make sentences.**

1 science lab | is | the | in the | working | scientist
The scientist is working in the science lab.

2 are | the children | in the | What | doing | river?

3 friends | having | My | in the | aren't | canteen | lunch

4 the car | Mum | to the | taking | mechanic | is

5 in the | playing | the musician | theatre | Is | the piano?

4 **Read and write *True* or *False* for you. Then write two more rules.**

1 You must wear a uniform. _____
2 You mustn't have lunch at school. _____
3 You must study English at school. _____
4 You mustn't be late for school. _____
5 _____
6 _____

Vocabulary and Grammar reference

1 **Translate the words into your language. Add more words to the list.**

Jobs

actor _____

actress _____

bus driver _____

chef _____

farmer _____

firefighter _____

mechanic _____

musician _____

police officer _____

scientist _____

singer _____

vet _____

waiter _____

waitress _____

_____ _____

_____ _____

_____ _____

Rules

arrive on time _____

be late _____

be quiet in class _____

break the rules _____

drop litter _____

follow the rules _____

put litter in the bin _____

shout in class _____

_____ _____

_____ _____

_____ _____

Grammar

2 **Read and complete.**

am   I̶   Is   're   isn't   flying   playing

Present continuous: Affirmative and Negative		
¹ _I_	'm / 'm not	singing a song.
He/She/It	's / ² _____	³ _____ a kite.
We/You/They	⁴ _____ / aren't	having lunch.

Present continuous: Questions			Short answers
Am	I	⁵ _____ the piano?	Yes, I ⁶ _____ . / No, I'm not.
⁷ _____	he/she/it	washing the car?	Yes, he/she/it is. / No, he/she/it isn't.
Are	we/you/they	feeding the cat?	Yes, we/you/they are. / No, we/you/they aren't.

Get ready for...

A1 Movers Reading and Writing Part 3

Think! **1** **Read and complete the sentences.**

easy ~~mechanic~~ drinking favourite zoo
difficult eating school actor exciting

1 Elias is a _____*mechanic*_____. He works with cars.

2 Paola is _____ orange juice.

3 I can't do _____ exercises.

4 My friends always arrive on time at _____.

5 This is a very _____ film.

Do! **2** 🎯 **Read. Choose a word from the box. Write the correct word next to numbers 1–6.**

farmer   delicious   listening   dangerous

cows   zoo   cooking   chef

Hi! I'm Diana. I love going to school. Today I want to tell you about our class jobs book. Do you know what it is? Well … it's a book with all the jobs our family do. And this is my family!

This is my mum Sally. She's a zoo vet. She works in the **(1)** __*zoo*__ and helps animals when they're ill.

This is my dad Oliver. He's a **(2)**_____. He works in a restaurant. In this picture he's **(3)**_____ toad-in-the-hole with me!

This is my uncle Harry. He's a firefighter. I think it's a **(4)**_____ job, but he says it's exciting.

This is my aunt Susan. She's a musician. She plays the piano very well. In this picture she's **(5)**_____ to music. She's a music teacher, too.

And these are our cousins Nicola and Tom. They're farmers. They've got some **(6)**_____ and Nicola gives us fresh milk every day! They've also got some sheep and horses, too.

5 Hobbies

Vocabulary

1 Look at Pupil's Book page 60 and answer.

1 What are the boy and girl sitting at the picnic table doing? _____

They're playing chess. _____

2 Which costumes are the children trying on? _____

3 What water sports can you see? _____

2 Look and write.

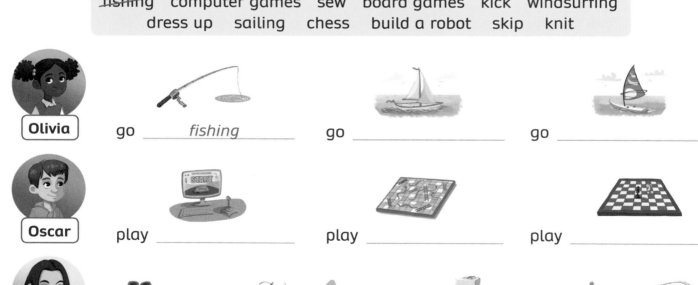

~~fishing~~   computer games   sew   board games   kick   windsurfing
dress up   sailing   chess   build a robot   skip   knit

Olivia   go ___ _fishing_ ___   go _____   go _____

Oscar   play _____   play _____   play _____

Emily

_____   _____   _____   _____   _____   _____

3 What are they doing? Look at Activity 2 and write _True_ or _False_.

1 Olivia's playing chess.   _False_

2 Oscar's skipping.   _____

3 Emily's building a toy house.   _____

4 Oscar's playing computer games.   _____

5 Emily's going fishing.   _____

6 Olivia's going sailing.   _____

1 After you read **Look, read and match. Then order.**

a

What's a nest?

I'd rather go windsurfing.

1

c

b

Help! I can't get out!

Bo, can you bring the baby bird up to the nest?

d

2 🔍 **What activities can you see on the map in Picture a?**

_____ _____ _____ _____

3 **Complete the sentences. Which is the extra word?**

windsurfing bird scared ~~climbing~~ monster nest help

1 The children decide to go _____*climbing*_____ first.

2 A baby _____ can't get back to its house in the tree.

3 Lottie wants Bo to take the baby bird up to its _____.

4 Bo is _____ because he thinks there is a _____ inside the hole.

5 The children _____ Bo.

4 Values **Read and tick (✓). How do you protect animals?**

1 Oh, no! The baby bird is hurt. Let's look for help. ✓

2 Here's a nest. Let's take it home! ☐

3 Don't make noise in the forest. ☐

4 Let's climb up to that nest and take the eggs! ☐

5 Don't leave rubbish in the forest. Take it home with you. ☐

Grammar

1 🎧 5.4 **Listen and match. Write.**

Grammar reference, page 66

a ✓ ✗

b ✗ ✗

c ✓ ✓

d ✗ ✓

e ✗ ✓

Henry

f ✗ ✗

Henry
Samuel
Jessica
Mia
Logan
Grace

2 💡 **Look at Activity 1. Who can't do the same thing? Write.**

_____ , _____ and _____ can't _____

3 **Write the questions and match the answers.**

1 Henry / sew   _Can Henry sew_ _____ ? | e | **a** No, he can't.

2 Mia / play chess _____ ? | | | **b** Yes, she can.

3 Jessica / knit _____ ? | | | **c** No, they can't.

4 Samuel / skip _____ ? | | | **d** No, she can't.

5 Henry and Grace / kick the ball _____ ? | | | **e** Yes, he can.

6 Logan and Henry / sew _____ ? | | | **f** Yes, they can.

4 **Write two things you can do and two things you can't do.**

I can _____ and _____ .

I can't _____ or _____ .

1 **Look and write.**

~~slowly~~ quietly badly well easily carefully quickly loudly

1 *slowly*

2 _ a _ _ _ _

3 _ _ _ _ _ _ _ l _ y

4 _ _ s _ _ _ _

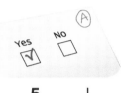

5 _ _ _ l

6 _ _ u _ _ _

7 _ _ _ k _ _

8 _ _ _ e _ _ _ _

2 **Look at Activity 1. Can you find pairs?**

1 _____ *slowly, quickly* _____   **2** _____   **3** _____

3 🎧 5.9 **Listen and match.**

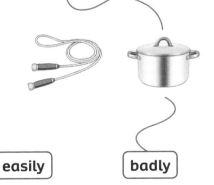

Claire   Zack   Lucy   Jim and Grace    Oliver and Paul   Sasha and Amy

easily   badly   quickly   slowly   loudly   well

4 **Look at Activity 3 and complete.**

1 Claire _____ *can cook badly* _____ .

2 Lucy _____ .

3 Zack _____ .

4 Sasha and Amy _____ .

5 Oliver and Paul _____ .

6 Jim and Grace _____ .

»» Extra practice, page 65

CULTURE

1 **Complete the bubble web.**

use a bat   run quickly   diamond   kick the ball   wicket

use a bat

_____

_____

Cricket

_____

Baseball

Australian Rules Football

_____

I'm learning

Make your own bubble web. Try other topics such as subjects at school, sports or food.

2 After you read **Complete the sentences with one, two or three words.**

high   hard   ~~baseball~~   bat   can   and   a   very   wicket   with   play

1 Many people ___ _play baseball_ ___ in the USA and in Japan.
2 In baseball you hit the ball _____.
3 The cricket ball is _____ and fast.
4 In cricket, you must run from wicket to _____.
5 In Australian Rules Football, players _____ kick the ball.
6 You can see players jumping _____.

3 **Think of a sport you play at school and answer.**

1 What sport is it? _____
2 How many players can play? _____
3 What do you need to play it? _____
4 Can you play it well? _____
5 What rules are there? Write two. _____
_____

1 (5.14) **Listen and tick (✓) what they would rather do.**

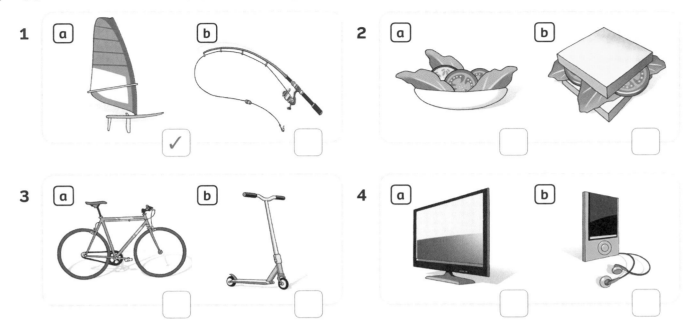

2 **Complete the dialogue.**

good idea   want to   I'd rather   ~~shall~~

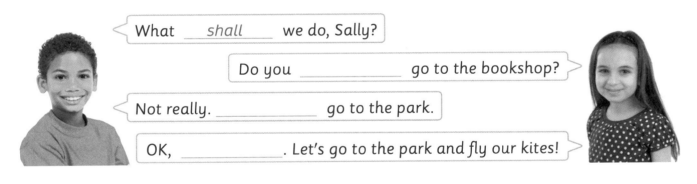

What ___shall___ we do, Sally?

Do you _____ go to the bookshop?

Not really. _____ go to the park.

OK, _____. Let's go to the park and fly our kites!

3 💬 **In pairs, talk about what you want to do together. Look at the pictures in Activity 1 or use your own ideas.**

Pronunciation

4 (5.15) **Colour the words with the /əʊ/ sound. Then listen and check.**

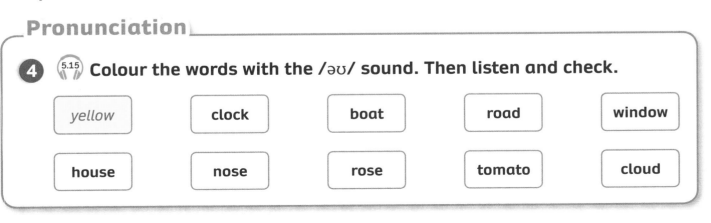

| yellow | clock | boat | road | window |
| house | nose | rose | tomato | cloud |

Reading

1 `After you read` **Look and read. Choose the correct word and write.**

cost

race

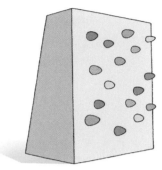

climbing wall

safety harness

arts and crafts

trampoline

1 You can learn climbing here.   _climbing wall_

2 The money you need to pay for something.   _____

3 You wear this when you go climbing or trampolining.   _____

4 Many people running at the same time.   _____

5 You use it to jump very high.   _____

6 You can make many creative things if you
   do this activity.   _____

2 **Circle the correct word.**

1 The Give-it-a-go Day is (at the weekend)/ in the week.

2 You can climb a tree / wall on the Give-it-a-go Day.

3 You can't run in a race in the morning / evening.

4 You can / can't make something with your hands.

5 The Give-it-a-go Day is in a park / leisure centre.

6 You pay three pounds for three activities / everything you do.

Writing

1 Read and match.

1 First name:
2 Surname:
3 Date of birth:
4 Address:
5 Home phone number:
6 Emergency contact:
7 Relationship:
8 Any allergies?
9 Taking part in:

a FLOWERS
b LILLY
c ANNE SULLIVAN
d SULLIVAN
e MOTHER
f CHESS, SWIMMING
g 15/01/2010
h 23 REGENT STREET, ELY
i 1229 324354

tip Writing

Use capital letters when you fill in a form.

2 Fill in your own form.

1 Plan

Read and answer. Make notes.

Who's your emergency contact? _____

What's his/her phone number? _____

Do you have any allergies? _____

2 Write

Use your notes and write. Then draw.

First name: _____   Emergency contact: _____

Surname: _____   Relationship: _____

Date of birth: _____   Any allergies? _____

Address: _____   Taking part in: _____

Home phone number: _____   _____

3 Check your work ✓

Read your form again and tick (✓).

All in capital letters? ☐   Correct spelling? ☐   Clear handwriting? ☐

3 Design your own form and take it home. Ask your family to fill it in.

1  **What can or can't your family do? Complete the table.**

go fishing   play chess   play board games   skip   knit   sew   play computer games
go windsurfing   kick a ball   build a robot   go sailing   sing   dance
play the guitar   cook   ride a bike   play tennis   skateboard

well   easily   badly   carefully   slowly   quickly   loudly   quietly

Family	can	can't
Me		

2 **Look at Activity 1 and write.**

I can play chess well but I can't play the piano quickly.

_____

_____

_____

_____

_____

_____

_____

_____

Self-evaluation

My work in Unit 5 is OK / good / excellent.

My favourite lesson is the one about _____.

Now I can _____.

I need to work more on _____.

1 Complete the missing letters. Use *a, e, i, o* or *u*.

1 g_o_ fishing
2 pl_y ch_ss
3 sk_p
4 g_ s__l_ng

5 b__ld _ r_b_t
6 g_ w_nds_rf_ng
7 s_w
8 pl_y c_mp_t_r g_m_s

9 k_ck
10 dr_ss _p
11 kn_t
12 pl_y b__rd g_m_s

2 Follow the lines and write. Use *can* or *can't*.

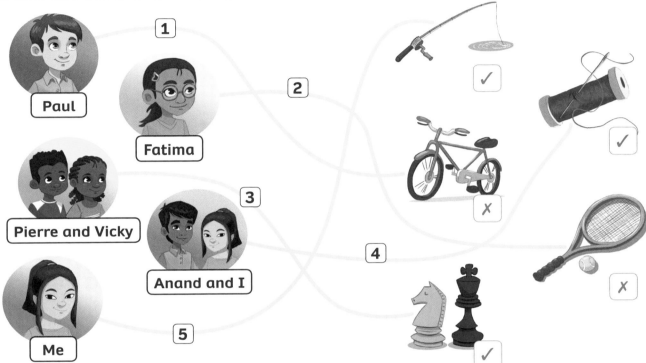

1 Paul *can't ride a bike* _____.
2 Fatima _____.
3 Pierre and Vicky _____.
4 Anand and I _____.
5 I _____.

3 Write about what you can or can't do.

carefully well loudly quietly ~~quickly~~ slowly easily badly

1 run ____*I can run quickly.*____
2 sing _____
3 read _____

4 paint _____
5 knit _____
6 play chess _____

Vocabulary and Grammar reference

Vocabulary

1 **Translate the words into your language. Add more words to the list.**

Hobbies and free time

build a robot _____

dress up _____

go fishing _____

go sailing _____

go windsurfing _____

kick _____

knit _____

play board games _____

play chess _____

play computer games _____

sew _____

skip _____

_____ _____

Adverbs

badly _____

carefully _____

easily _____

loudly _____

quickly _____

quietly _____

slowly _____

well _____

_____

_____

_____

_____

Grammar

2 **Read and complete.**

What   well   quick   can't   knit   reads   Can   loudly   ~~speak~~

Can – Affirmative and negative

I	can [1] _speak_	English.
He/She/It		
We/You/They	[2]_____ play	tennis.

Can – Questions

[3]_____	can	I	do?
		he/she/it	
		we/you/they	
[4]_____	I		sing?
	he/she/it		
	we/you/they		

Regular adverbs

[5]_____	+ ly →	quickly	I run very quickly.
careful		carefully	He [7]_____ carefully.
loud		[6]_____	She speaks loudly.

Irregular adverbs

| good → | [8]_____ | They [9]_____ well. |

Get ready for...

A1 Movers Reading and Writing Part 6

Think! ❶ **What can you see in the picture in Activity 2? Tick (✓).**

a boy windsurfing ☐	a yellow T-shirt ☐	a kite ☐
trees ☐	a lake ☐	a river ☐
a girl skipping ☐	ice creams ☐	a boy sailing ☐
a blue T-shirt ☐	a teddy bear ☐	a football ☐

Do! ❷ 🎯 **Look and read and write.**

Complete the sentences.

1 The girl is windsurfing in the _____*lake*_____ .

2 The boy and girl in blue T-shirts are playing _____ .

Answer the questions.

3 What's the girl with the kite wearing? _____ .

4 What food can you buy in the park? _____ .

Now write two sentences about the picture.

5 _____ .

6 _____ .

Our town

Vocabulary

1 🕐 **Look at Pupil's Book page 72 and answer.**

1 What's the man sitting in the boat doing?   *He's fishing.*

2 Is the musician playing the piano?   _____

3 What's to the left of the café?   _____

2 **Look and write.**

> bridge market shopping centre café square theatre
> hotel clothes shop train station bus stop ~~zoo~~ car park

zoo

3 **Answer the questions with words from Activity 2.**

1 Where can I sleep?   *hotel*

2 Where can I buy food?   _____

3 Where can I take the bus?   _____

4 Where can I see an actress?   _____

5 Where can I have a hot drink?   _____

4 💬 **Which places from Activity 2 do you go to at the weekend? Compare in pairs.**

1 After you read **Read and complete. Then match.**

problem   coming   wall   ~~square~~   river

1 There's a deep flood in the _____square_____ in Barhaven.

2 150 years ago, there was a _____ next to the square.

3 The Discovery Team thinks the river is the _____.

4 Bo finds that the underground _____ is broken.

5 The Discovery Team finds out where the flood is _____ from.

2 **Read and write *True* or *False*.**

1 It's a sunny day in Barhaven. _____False_____

2 The children are doing a Social Science project about Barhaven. _____

3 150 years ago there was a zoo in Barhaven. _____

4 Lois goes down to the underground river. _____

5 The roads in Barhaven are under the rivers. _____

3 **Correct the false sentences in Activity 2.**

_____It's a rainy day in Barhaven._____   _____

_____   _____

4 Values **Read and tick (✓). How do you work together?**

1 Come and help us with our project! ✓   **2** I can share my map with you. ☐

3 Let's go to the library together. ☐   **4** I don't like your idea. ☐

Grammar

1 🎯 🎧6.5 **Listen and tick (✓).**

Grammar reference, page 78

1 Who was at the theatre last week?

2 Where were Zoe and Sally yesterday?

3 Which was the most difficult exam?

4 When was Alan's party?

2 **Complete the questions with *was* or *were*.**

1 Where _____*were*_____ Jane and Alex two days ago?

2 _____ Jane at the market last Monday?

3 _____ Jane and Alex at the clothes shop last Wednesday?

4 Where _____ you and Alex last Tuesday?

3 **Today is Sunday. Look and answer the questions in Activity 2.**

Monday	Tuesday	Wednesday	Thursday	Friday	Saturday	Sunday
Jane	Alex and I	Jane and Alex	Jane	Jane and Alex	Alex	

1 Jane and Alex _____*were at the bank*_____ two days ago.

2 _____, she _____. She _____.

3 _____, they _____. They _____.

4 We _____.

Vocabulary and Grammar

1 Look, match and write.

cheap   ancient   ~~noisy~~   safe

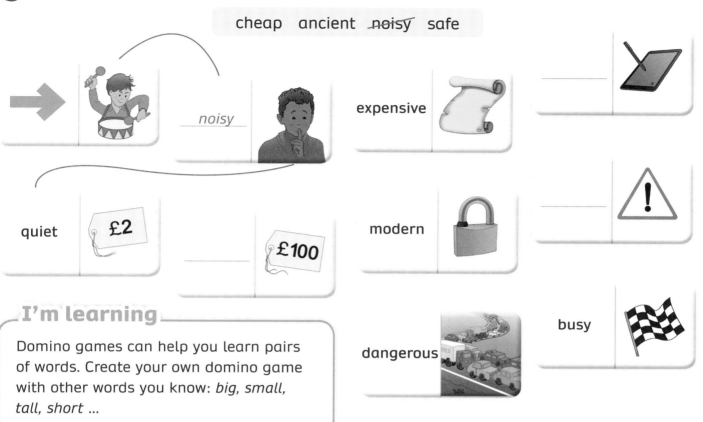

noisy

quiet   £2

expensive

modern

dangerous

busy

I'm learning

Domino games can help you learn pairs of words. Create your own domino game with other words you know: *big, small, tall, short* …

2 Look and tick (✓) or cross (✗). Then complete the sentences.

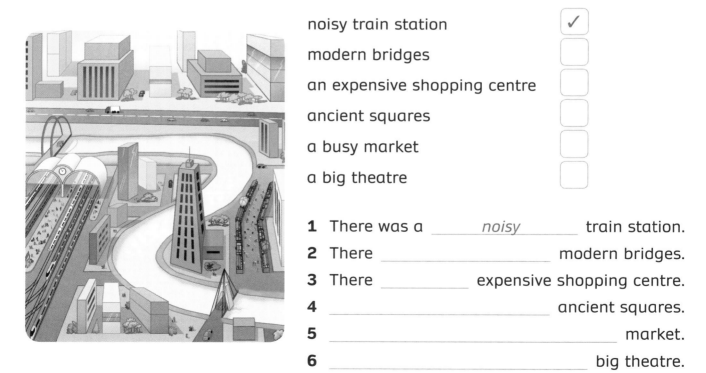

noisy train station ✓

modern bridges

an expensive shopping centre

ancient squares

a busy market

a big theatre

1 There was a _____noisy_____ train station.

2 There _____ modern bridges.

3 There _____ expensive shopping centre.

4 _____ ancient squares.

5 _____ market.

6 _____ big theatre.

Extra practice, page 77

CULTURE

1 Look and number.

modern ☐ ☐   ancient ☐   views ☐   theatre ☐ ☐   tower [1]

2 After you read Match the sentence halves.

a is an ancient Roman theatre.

1 The CN Tower

b looks like a boat.

c was the tallest tower in the world for many years.

2 The Colosseum

d was very noisy inside.

e has got a restaurant at the top.

3 Sydney Opera House

f is the most famous building in the country.

3 Read and choose.

1 The CN tower is the most ancient / modern building and the Colosseum is the most ancient / modern.

2 I think the Sydney Opera House is taller / more famous than the CN Tower, but the Colosseum is the most famous / quietest of all.

English in action
Making recommendations

1 🎯 **Read and choose the best answer.**

1 Where were you yesterday?
  a Yes, I was.
  b No, there wasn't any.
  c I was at the new café.

2 You should go and see it.
  a Anything else?
  b Hey, Sandy!
  c Good idea!

3 How was it?
  a It was boring.
  b I was at the park.
  c Really?

4 What was the café like?
  a Yes, I like it very much.
  b It was nice and quiet.
  c No, it wasn't.

2 **Complete the dialogue with sentences 1–4 in Activity 1.**

Hey Alyssa, I was at the new café yesterday.

Really? _What was the café like?_

It was beautiful and clean, but it was very busy. _____

I was at the new market yesterday.

_____

There was a lot of noise, but the fruit was delicious. _____

Good idea!

3 **In pairs, ask and answer.**

1 Where were you last Saturday? _____

2 What was it like? _____

3 Was it boring or exciting? _____

Pronunciation

4 🎧 (6.14) **Read and colour the words. Use brown for the /uː/ sound and yellow for the /ɜː/ sound. Then listen and check. What can you see?**

I can see a pair of _____.

bird | zoo | turkey | roof | skirt | shoe | girl | blue | dirty | burger | you | fur | school | fruit | glue

---

Reading

---

1 **After you read** **Complete the table.**

~~smaller~~   car parks   bigger   a lot of markets   a lot of horses
a lot of bridges   no trains   cinemas   The Bosphorus   one bridge

Istanbul	
400 years ago	**Now**
smaller	

2 💡 **Look at the table. Find two things in common.**

_____   _____

3 **Choose the correct answer.**

1 Today Istanbul is smaller /(bigger) than 400 years ago.

2 The Bosphorus was very quiet / busy 400 years ago.

3 In the past, people used horses / cars to travel around Istanbul.

4 The Great Fire was in 1660 / 1666.

5 The Bosphorus Bridge / Galata Bridge was the only bridge across the
Bosphorus in Istanbul.

4 👥 **Look at Activity 1. In groups, make a big poster of Istanbul then and now.**

Writing

1 Look at the pictures and write. Choose an adjective from Box A and then choose an adjective from Box B.

A big long ~~beautiful~~ small   **B** orange busy ancient ~~modern~~

1 a ___*beautiful, modern*___ town   **2** a _____ kite

3 a _____ bridge   **4** a _____ market

2 Write about your town or city in the past.

1 Plan

Read and answer. Make notes.

What's the name of your town or city? _____

What was there 500 years ago? _____

What can you see there now? _____

2 Write

Use your notes and write.

My town then and now

Hi, my name's _____.   I live in _____.

500 years ago, there _____

_____

_____

Today, there _____

_____

_____

3 Check your work ✔

Read your text again and tick (✓).

Commas between adjectives? ☐   Correct spelling? ☐   Clear handwriting? ☐

1 **Look, read and circle the correct word.**

@Kim

My name's Ilhan. Look at this picture! I **(1)** was / wasn't
in a new **(2)** city / café with my family last weekend.
It **(3)** were / was a quiet place. There **(4)** were / weren't
a lot of noisy roads. There was a **(5)** modern / high
market. The food was very cheap. We were at the
(6) zoo / shopping centre, too. It was very interesting.
There were a lot of big, dangerous animals. The **(7)** food / building wasn't exciting: there were
only cheese sandwiches, but they were **(8)** difficult / delicious! I love visiting new cities!

2 **Where were you last weekend or last month? Draw and write.**

My name's _____.
Look at this picture! I was in _____.
It was _____.
There were _____
_____.
There weren't _____
_____
_____.
The food _____.
_____.
I love visiting new cities!

Self-evaluation

My work in Unit 6 is OK / good / excellent.
My favourite lesson is the one about _____.
Now I can _____.
I need to work more on _____.

1 Match the words and pictures.

1 fruit	a park
2 clothes	b station
3 shopping	c market
4 train	d stop
5 car	e shop
6 bus	f centre

2 Complete the missing letters.

1 z o o   3 h _ t _ l   5 br _ dg _

2 c _ f _   4 th _ _ tr _   6 sq _ _ r _

3 Choose the correct answer and write.

1 Gina and Sally was / were at the _____theatre_____ yesterday.

2 My parents wasn't / weren't at the _____ last Saturday.

3 Was / Were the car on the _____?

4 The children was / were at the _____.

5 Were / Was you and Sam at the _____? No, we wasn't / weren't.

4 Imagine a town or city in the past. Write sentences.

noisy cheap safe modern expensive quiet ancient busy	street restaurant road building café bridge shop

1 There was _____.

2 There wasn't _____.

3 There were _____.

4 There weren't _____.

Vocabulary and Grammar reference

Vocabulary

1 **Translate the words into your language. Add more words to the list.**

Places in town		Adjectives	
bridge	_____	ancient	_____
bus stop	_____	busy	_____
café	_____	cheap	_____
car park	_____	expensive	_____
clothes shop	_____	modern	_____
hotel	_____	noisy	_____
market	_____	quiet	_____
shopping centre	_____	safe	_____
square	_____		_____
theatre	_____		_____
train station	_____		_____
zoo	_____		_____

Grammar

2 **Read and complete.**

Was   ~~wasn't~~   ago   you   wasn't   There   weren't   yesterday   were   Where

Was/Were – Affirmative and negative			
I He/She/It	was/ [1] _wasn't_	at the zoo	yesterday. a week [2] _____. last Saturday.
We/You/They	were/weren't		
[3] _____	was/wasn't	an ancient bridge.	
	were/ [4] _____	a lot of busy markets.	

Was/Were – Interrogative and short answers			
[5] _____	was	I he/she/it	[6] _____ ?
	were	we/you/they	
	[7] _____	I he/she/it	at the café?
	Were	we/ [8] _____ /they	
Yes, I/he/she/it was. / Yes, we/you/they [9] _____.			
No, I/he/she/it [10] _____. /No, we/you/they weren't.			

Get ready for...

A1 Movers Listening Part 2

Think! **1** **Match the words with the headings.**

theatres   busy   bridges   noisy   safe   quiet

Types of transport   **Types of buildings/places**   **Words to describe a city**

cars   trains   houses   markets   buses   bikes

Do! **2** **Listen and write.**

Our city

1 Homework is about: Our city in the _____*past*_____

2 Number of different types of buildings: _____

3 The most important building: _____

4 Name of cinema: _____

5 Transport in the city: _____

6 The streets weren't: _____

Language booster 2

1 **Find and circle the words.**

c	a	r	e	f	u	l	m
n	s	b	c	f	o	c	p
v	y	v	l	b	u	b	r
e	n	z	a	a	x	r	e
s	l	o	w	d	j	a	t
q	e	j	k	f	z	v	t
y	g	s	i	t	b	e	y
q	r	h	o	d	p	w	v
n	a	u	g	h	t	y	l

2 **Look, read and circle.**

1 It's bad / pretty.

2 The old car is brave / slow.

3 The cat is careful / naughty.

4 He's brave / pretty.

3 **Complete the sentences with words from Activity 1.**

1 I love my new dress. It's _____pretty_____.

2 My dad is a firefighter. He's very _____.

3 My dog eats our shoes. It's _____.

4 My pet tortoise isn't fast. It's _____.

5 When I cross the road, I'm always _____.

6 The film wasn't good. It was _____.

4 **Match the speech bubbles to the pictures.**

1 I want you to carry the shopping.

2 I want you to be very careful!

3 I want you to dress up as a pirate!

4 I want you to run quickly.

a

b

c

d

5 **Order the words to make sentences.**

1 She / me / wants / carry / the / to / shopping.

_____

2 to / be / wants / me / careful. / Mum

_____

3 dress up. / My sister / to / wants / me

_____

4 wants / us / The teacher / run / to / quickly!

_____

6 **What do they want you to do? Write and draw.**

1 My mum wants me to

_____ _____.

2 My teacher wants me to

_____ _____.

3 My friend wants me to

_____ _____.

4 My brother / sister wants me to

_____ _____.

7 In Roman times

Vocabulary

1 ⏱ **Look at Pupil's Book page 88 and answer.**

1 What have the two men next to the door got in their hands?
They've got shields.

2 What's next to the cupcakes? _____

3 What are Ash, Lois and Lottie doing? _____

2 **Complete the crossword. What's the secret phrase?**

helmet   mosaic   coins   wall   jewellery   jugs   necklace   shield   *ring*

| 1 | R | I | N | G |

2

3

4

5

6

7

M

8

9

3 💡 **Read and write a sentence with the words and your own ideas.**

1 | iron | | necklace | *This necklace is made of iron. It's beautiful.*

2 | stone | | wall | _____

3 | stone | | mosaic | _____

4 | iron | | coins | _____

5 | clay | | jugs | _____

I'm learning

It's good to learn new words by making sentences.

1 `After you read` **Look, read and order.**

The discovery

2 **Answer the questions.**

1 Where are the children? _____ *They're outside the museum.*

2 What was the name of Barhaven in Roman times? _____

3 What can Lois see on her tablet? _____

4 What's the object that Lois finds made of? _____

5 What do they finally find? _____

3 **What does the mosaic look like? Tick (✓).**

1 It's got hair. ☐

2 It's red and black. ☐

3 It's got snakes. ✓

4 It's red and blue. ☐

5 There's a head. ☐

6 It's an animal. ☐

4 `Values` **Read and tick (✓). When are you careful?**

1 doing homework ☐

2 crossing the road ☐

3 dancing ☐

4 playing computer games ☐

5 cooking ☐

6 sewing ☐

1 🎧 7.5 **Listen and circle.**

Grammar reference, page 92

1

Alan

watch TV
(tidy up his bedroom)

(on Monday)
on Tuesday

2

Jessy

watch a film at the cinema
watch a film at home

last Friday
last Saturday

3

Tom and Henry

paint a picture
play tennis

two days ago
yesterday

4

Sally and Alice

climb
skateboard

two days ago
yesterday

5

Julia and Bill

play baseball
play board games

last week
last weekend

2 **Look at Activity 1 and complete the sentences.**

1 Alan didn't _____watch TV_____ on Monday. He _____tidied up_____ his bedroom.

2 Jessy didn't _____. She _____.

3 Tom and Henry didn't _____. They _____.

4 Sally and Alice didn't _____. They _____.

5 Julia and Bill _____. _____.

3 💬 **Guess what your partner did yesterday. Tick (✓) or cross (✗). Then say and check.**

walk to school ☐   watch TV ☐   tidy up your room ☐

play football ☐   listen to music ☐   dance ☐

You walked to school.   No, I didn't walk to school. I took the bus.

1 Complete the sentences.

live   work   visit   arrive   start   stop   need   ~~use~~

1 I always _____*use*_____ a pen to write at school.

2 You _____ a sentence with a capital letter.

3 I _____ in a flat in the city centre.

4 I _____ my grandparents every weekend.

5 My parents _____ in a shop.

6 Trains often _____ on time at the train station.

7 I can't see. I _____ my glasses.

8 Shh! Please, _____ talking. This is a library.

2 Order the words to make questions.

1 Ben   place   What   visit   did
on Saturday   ?   _____*What place did Ben visit on Saturday?*_____

2 arrive   time   did   What   Ben   ?   _____

3 to buy   Ben   What   did   need   ?   _____

4 the woman   What   use
to take photos   did   ?   _____

5 touch   Did   the shield   the girls   ?   _____

3 🎯 Look and answer the questions in Activity 2.

1 _*He visited a museum on Saturday.*_

2 _____

3 _____

4 _____

5 _____

CULTURE

1 After you read **Complete the table.**

on the floor   ~~hot water baths~~   have a lot of small pieces
135 kilometres long   Aquae Sulis   keep out the Picts

Bath	Hadrian's Wall	Mosaics
hot water baths		

2 **Answer the questions.**

1 How long did the Romans live in Britain?   *They lived in Britain for 400 years.*

2 What's the modern name of Aquae Sulis?   _____

3 Where was Hadrian's Wall?   _____

4 Who was Hadrian?   _____

5 Where can you find Roman mosaics?   _____

3 **Order the pieces to make a sentence.**

THE RO
ER FOR   HOT WAT
ED THE   MANS US
FUL BA   BEAUTI
THS.

The Romans _____

4 **Look at Activity 3. Write a 'broken' sentence for your partner.**

English in action
Giving advice

1 (7.14) **Write *should* or *shouldn't*. Then listen and number.**

a   b   c

d   e   f

a   You ___should___ listen to your teacher. ☐

b   You _____ run in the classroom. ☐

c   You _____ drop litter. ☐

d   You _____ shout in class. ☐

e   You _____ clean your table. ☐

f   You _____ arrive on time. ☐ *1*

2 **Complete the dialogue.**

~~how to work~~   Should we   should I do   You should   No

Hello, my name's Jian and I work at the library. Today we're learning about ___how to work___ and study here with the new students.

Hi Paul. What _____ ?

_____ read and talk very quietly. You should take care of the books.

_____ put the books back on this table?

Good question! _____, you shouldn't. You should put them back on the shelves.

3 💬 **Choose and complete for you. Then compare in groups.**

When you go to the theatre / zoo / café / library, you should _____

_____. You shouldn't _____.

Pronunciation

4 (7.15) **Complete the table. Then listen and check.**

~~tall~~   water   Art   floor   aunt   bored   arms   park

/ɔː/	tall			
/ɑː/				

Reading

1 **After you read** **Read and write.**

winner   diary   show   ~~Colosseum~~   outside   battle

1 A very big theatre in Rome.

_____Colosseum_____

2 When you are not inside, you are …

_____

3 Something you watch at a theatre.

_____

4 You write about your everyday routine in a …

_____

5 When two groups of people don't like each other, this may happen.

_____

6 When you finish first in a race you are the …

_____

2 **Read and write _True_ or _False_.**

1 Marcus is twelve years old.   _False_

2 Tito is Marcus' dog.   _____

3 The Colosseum was very quiet.   _____

4 Marcus watched a show with a lion and a tiger.   _____

5 The Britons painted their faces blue in the battle in the Colosseum.   _____

6 The Britons were the winners of the battle.   _____

3 **Correct the false sentences in Activity 2.**

Marcus is eleven years old.

_____

_____

_____

_____

7

Writing

tip **Writing**
Use adjectives to show how you feel and to make your writing more interesting!

1 **Read and complete.**

boring   exciting   dangerous   ~~ancient~~

1 I visited a castle last Thursday. It was a _ncient_____.

2 I was in Mexico City last week. It was so e_____!

3 I didn't like the Maths lesson last week. It was b_____.

4 She climbed a very high wall yesterday. It was so d_____.

2 **Write a diary about a visit to a new place.**

1 Plan

Read and answer. Make notes.

What day is it? _____

What's your name, how old are you and where do you live? _____

_____

When did you arrive? _____

What did you visit? _____

What was it like? _____

2 Write

Use your notes and write.

My diary

My name is _____.

I'm _____.

I live in _____

_____.

Today we _____

_____

_____.

In the morning we _____

_____.

Then we_____

_____.

It was_____

_____

_____.

3 Check your work ✔

Read your text again and tick (✓).

Use at least three adjectives? ☐   Correct spelling? ☐   Clear handwriting? ☐

1 Look, read and complete the text.

Jewellery workshop

We ___arrived___ (arrive) at 10 o'clock in the morning and _____ (start) our workshop. First we _____ (use) **(1)** ___clay___ to make some **(2)** _____ . We _____ (not use) **(3)** _____ because it was more difficult. We _____ (work) for two hours and then we _____ (stop) for thirty minutes. We _____ (not play) football, but we _____ (skip) in the playground. Then we _____ (paint) our **(2)** _____ and _____ (tidy up) the room. We _____ (finish) at 2 o'clock. My **(4)** _____ and my **(5)** _____ were really beautiful!

2 Write about a Roman costume workshop. Use the words in the box.

iron   shield   stone   helmet   dress   wood

ROMAN COSTUME WORKSHOP

We arrived at _____ .

First we used _____ .

_____

We worked for _____ .

_____

Then we _____ .

We finished at _____ . My _____ was/were really _____ !

Self-evaluation

My work in Unit 7 is OK / good / excellent.

My favourite lesson is the one about _____ .

Now I can _____ .

I need to work more on _____ .

1 **Read and write.**

> iron jewellery jug coins ring stone
> helmet clay necklace shield mosaic walls

1 I can wear it: _jewellery_ , _____ , _____ , _____ , _____

2 I can use it to make things: _____ , _____ , _____

3 I can pay with it: _____

4 I can put water in it: _____

5 Around my house there are: _____

6 I can decorate a house with it: _____

2 **Can you think of more words for each category in Activity 1?**

1 _____   **3** _____   **5** _____

2 _____   **4** _____   **6** _____

3 **Find and circle eight verbs and write them in the Past simple.**

workmlrstopferusevalneedpkyliveascarrivenigvisitdrestartthi

1 _worked_   **3** _____   **5** _____   **7** _____

2 _____   **4** _____   **6** _____   **8** _____

4 **Complete the sentences. Use the Past simple.**

1 We ___watched___ (watch) a very boring film yesterday.

2 My sister _____ (walk) to the beach last weekend.

3 I _____ (not wash) my mum's car last week.

4 Peter _____ (tidy up) his room two days ago, but
he _____ (not clean) the floor.

5 You _____ (not visit) the Roman museum on Monday.

5 **Answer the questions.**

1 Did you arrive late at school last week?   _____

2 Did you use your pencil to do Activity 1?   _____

3 What time did you start school on Monday?   _____

4 Did you work hard last term?   _____

Vocabulary and Grammar reference

Vocabulary

1 **Translate the words into your language. Add more words to the list.**

Roman times

coins _____

helmet _____

jewellery _____

jug _____

mosaic _____

necklace _____

ring _____

shield _____

wall _____

_____ _____

_____ _____

_____ _____

_____ _____

_____ _____

Materials

clay _____

iron _____

stone _____

_____

_____

Verbs

arrive _____

live _____

need _____

start _____

stop _____

use _____

visit _____

work _____

_____

_____

Grammar

2 **Read and complete.**

did   wash   like   didn't   ~~washed~~

Past simple – Affirmative and negative		
I He/She/It We/You/They	¹ _washed_ the car didn't ²_____ the car	yesterday. two days ago. last week.

Past simple – Interrogative and short answers		
Did		³_____ those cupcakes?
Yes,	I he/she/it we/you/they	did.
No,		⁴_____.
When ⁵_____		play baseball?

Get ready for...

A1 Movers Listening Part 3

Think! **1** Look at the pictures in Activity 2 and match.
Use the letters A–H.

go windsurfing	E	go climbing	☐	play chess	☐
learn arts and crafts	☐	play computer games	☐	go canoeing	☐
travel by train	☐	visit a museum	☐		

Do! **2** 🎯 🎧 7.18 Listen and write a letter in each box.

 1 Charlie (me) ☐

 A

B

 2 my granny D

C

D

 3 my aunt ☐

 E

F

4 my uncle ☐

5 my cousins ☐

G

H

 6 my brother ☐

8 Let's celebrate!

Vocabulary

1 🕐 **Look at Pupil's Book page 100 and write sentences about the picture.**

~~crisps~~   lake   party hats   rollercoaster

1 _____ *There are two bowls of crisps on the table at the party.*

2 _____

3 _____

4 _____

2 **Find, circle and write the words.**

webrideddinvitationingroomg   furollercoasternbigwheelfabandir   ppartygamesapartyhatrcostumety

bride

1 w_____

2 f_____

3 p_____

3 🎯 (8.3) **Listen and complete.**

1 Vicky's got _____ *an invitation* _____.

2 It's for Paul's birthday _____.

3 Vicky can wear a _____.

4 They can play party _____.

5 They can go to the _____ in town.

I'm learning

Your family photos can help you remember new words. Find photos from different celebrations and check how many people or things you can name in English. You can also find new words in a dictionary.

1 After you read **Look, read and match. Then circle. Who says what?**

The lost ring

a That's my jewellery box! ☐ Lottie / Lois / Ash / Grandad / Granny

b Have you still got your wedding dress? ☐ Lottie / Lois / Ash / Grandad / Granny

c Where did you get married, Grandad? [1] Lottie / (Lois) / Ash / Grandad / Granny

d In France, we lost the jewellery box. ☐ Lottie / Lois / Ash / Grandad / Granny

2 **Tick (✓) the things that are lost in the story.**

wedding ring [✓]   party hat ☐   jewellery box ☐

wedding dress ☐   wedding invitation ☐   a metal detector ☐

3 **Correct the mistakes.**

1 The children are at a <u>wedding</u> with Lottie and Lois' grandparents.   *funfair*

2 Lottie and Lois' grandparents got married in <u>Barhaven</u>.   _____

3 Granny has still got her wedding <u>invitation</u>.   _____

4 Lottie and Lois' grandparents lost the wedding ring in <u>Spain</u>.   _____

5 Bo helps them find the <u>toy box</u> with the ring in it.   _____

4 Values **What do you think? Read and choose.**

In the story, Lottie and Lois are learning about
sewing a wedding dress / their older family members' youth / being safe
at a funfair.

1 🎧 8.6 **Listen and tick (✓).**

Grammar reference, page 104

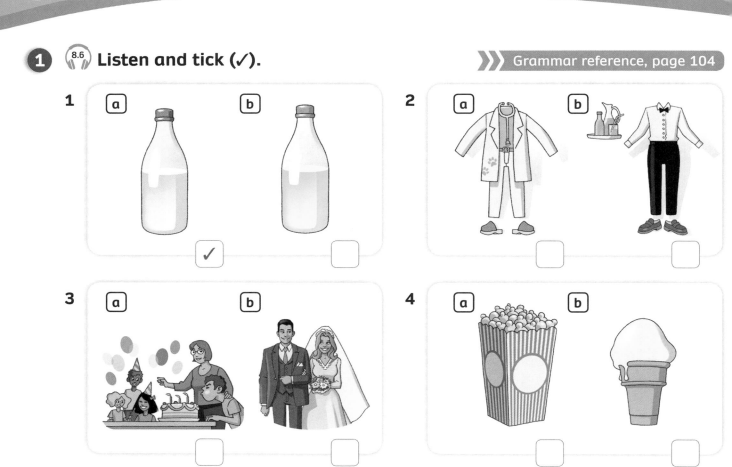

1
a   b ✓

2
a   b

3
a   b

4
a   b

2 **Look at Activity 1 and complete the sentences. Use the Past simple.**

go   eat   ~~drink~~   wear

1 Alex ___didn't drink___ lemonade. He ___drank___ water.

2 Alice _____ a vet costume. She _____ a waitress costume.

3 My family and I _____ to a birthday party. We _____ to a wedding.

4 Jill and Sarah _____ popcorn. They _____ ice cream.

3 💬 **Write three things you did and three things you didn't do yesterday. Compare in pairs.**

_____   _____

_____   _____

_____   _____

I drank milk.

I didn't eat chocolate.

Vocabulary and Grammar ⑧

1  **8.12 Listen and match. When is their birthday?**

Greg		30th		March
Sally		6th		January
Evie		1st		July
Carlos		19th		October

2 💡 **Look and read. When is their birthday? Write the dates in words.**

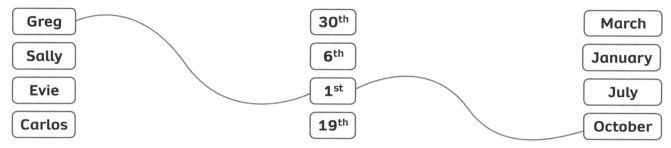

JUNE

	MONDAY	TUESDAY	WEDNESDAY	THURSDAY	FRIDAY	SATURDAY	SUNDAY
1					1st	2nd	3rd
2	4th	5th	6th	7th	8th	9th	10th
3	11th	12th	13th	14th	15th	16th	17th
4	18th	19th	20th	21st	22nd	23rd	24th
5	25th	26th	27th	28th	29th	30th	

1 I'm Michael. My birthday is in the fifth week of June.
It's on Friday. _____*twenty-ninth*_____

2 My mum's birthday is in the third week of June.
It's on the last day before the weekend. _____

3 I'm Rosa. My birthday is on the second Wednesday of June.
It's my lucky number. _____

4 Hi, I'm Naomi. My birthday is on a Thursday this year.
It's in the fourth week of June. _____

5 My sister's birthday this year is at the weekend.
It's the first Saturday in June. _____

3 **Complete the questions and answers.**

saw   drink   d̶i̶d̶n̶'̶t̶   D̶i̶d̶   Yes   give   did   eat   drank   see

1 _____*Did*_____ the bride wear a white dress? No, she _____*didn't*_____.

2 Did they _____ you the party invitation? Yes, they _____.

3 When did you _____ my parents? I _____ them yesterday.

4 Did the groom _____ the wedding cake? _____, he did.

5 What did your friends _____ at the cinema? They _____ lemonade.

Extra practice, page 103

CULTURE

1 **Match the words and dates to the festivals.**

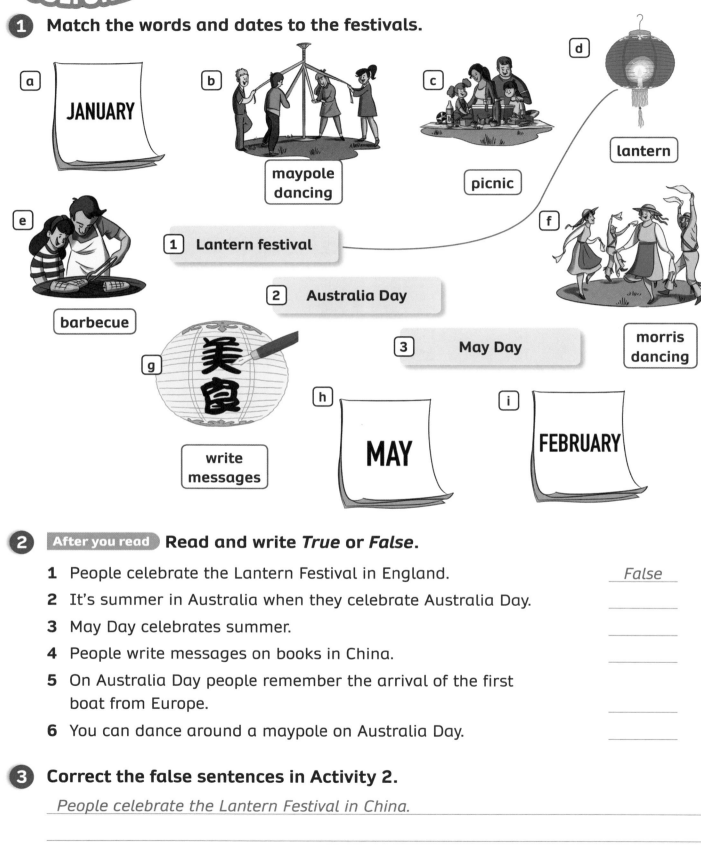

a JANUARY

b maypole dancing

c picnic

d lantern

e barbecue

1 Lantern festival

2 Australia Day

3 May Day

f morris dancing

g write messages

h MAY

i FEBRUARY

2 After you read **Read and write *True* or *False*.**

1 People celebrate the Lantern Festival in England. _____*False*_____

2 It's summer in Australia when they celebrate Australia Day. _____

3 May Day celebrates summer. _____

4 People write messages on books in China. _____

5 On Australia Day people remember the arrival of the first boat from Europe. _____

6 You can dance around a maypole on Australia Day. _____

3 **Correct the false sentences in Activity 2.**

People celebrate the Lantern Festival in China.

_____

_____

_____

English in action
Explaining you've lost something

8

1 **Order the words to make sentences.**

1 the what's matter ?   *What's the matter?*

2 . go there and let's look   _____

3 welcome you're !   _____

4 last when ? you did it see   _____

5 it like what's ?   _____

2 **Complete the dialogue with the sentences in Activity 1.**

> *What's the matter?*

> I can't find my necklace.

> _____

> It's made of metal and it's got a blue flower.

> _____

> Well… I had it when I went to our PE lesson.

> _____

> There it is! Thanks for your help!

> _____

Pronunciation

3 🎧 **8.17** **Colour the words with the /aʊ/ sound. Then listen and check.**

brown	famous	touch	cloudy
cow	bowl	window	stone
trousers	flower	go	canoe

Reading

1 **After you read** **Answer the questions.**

1 When was Yolanda's birthday party? _Yolanda's birthday party was at the weekend._

2 Where was her party? _____

3 What time did Yolanda's party start? _____

4 What time did Yolanda's party finish? _____

5 How many people were there? _____

6 What did everybody at the party wear? _____

7 What did they eat? _____

8 Where did they play party games? _____

9 Who is Patch? _____

10 Did Patch like the party? Why? _____

2 **Order the events in the story.**

They played more party games in the garden. ☐

Yolanda gave invitations to her friends. 1

There was no cake on the party table. ☐

They ate the party food. ☐

The dog ate the cake. ☐

Yolanda's friends came to her party. ☐

They played party games. ☐

They went back into the house to eat the cake. ☐

8

Writing

tip Writing

When you write the time, use *am/pm*.
10 am = in the morning.
10 pm = in the evening.
RSVP means *please reply*.

1 **Complete for yourself. Write the time. Use *am* or *pm*.**

1 When I go to school, I get up at _____ *7 am* _____ .

2 On Saturdays, I have dinner at _____ .

3 At the weekend, I go to bed at _____ .

4 School starts at _____ and finishes at _____ .

5 On Mondays, I have lunch at _____ .

6 At the weekend, I get up at _____ .

2 **Write an invitation to a party.**

1 Plan

Read and answer. Make notes.

Who are you inviting? _____

When is your party? _____

Where is it? _____

RSVP by? To an email or phone number? _____

2 Write

Use your notes and write. Then decorate the card.

To: _____

When: _____

Where: _____

RSVP by _____

to _____

Birthday Party

3 Check your work ✔

Read your text again and tick (✓).

Use *am* or *pm*? ☐   Use RSVP? ☐   Correct spelling? ☐   Clear handwriting? ☐

3 **Create your own party invitations and display them in class.**

1 Read Pat's review and answer her questionnaire.

Hi, I'm Pat. Yesterday it was Carnival at school. I didn't wear my school uniform. I dressed up as a pirate with my friend Tom. There was a parade and a band played some music. Before the parade we ate some party food. We didn't have ice creams because it was cold, but we had crisps, sandwiches and fruit. We drank some lemonade, too. After the parade we played some party games. It was fun!

School fancy dress parade!

1 What did she wear to school today?
  a a school uniform
  b PE clothes
  c a fancy dress costume

2 Who did she dress up with?
  a Tom
  b Carnival
  c Tia

3 She played music in a band.
  a True
  b False

4 What did she eat at school today?
  a fruit and ice cream
  b crisps, sandwiches and fruit
  c sandwiches and ice cream

5 She drank some lemonade.
  a True
  b False

6 She played some party games.
  a True
  b False

2 Write your own questionnaire for a fancy dress party. Use the words or your own ideas.

go   wear   eat   put   find   lose   have   make   see   get

Fancy dress party!

1 _____
  a _____
  b _____
2 _____
  a _____
  b _____

3 _____
  a _____
  b _____
4 _____
  a _____
  b _____

5 _____
  a _____
  b _____
6 _____
  a _____
  b _____

3 Give your questionnaire to your partner. Then tell the class about it.

Self-evaluation

My work in Unit 8 is OK / good / excellent.

My favourite lesson is the one about _____.

Now I can _____.

I need to work more on _____.

1 Write. Then match the words to the pictures.

party   invitation   coaster   ~~fun~~   big

1 _fun_ fair

2 _____ wheel

3 roller _____

4 wedding _____

5 _____ hat

2 Circle the correct word.

1 She (ate)/didn't eat a burger at Michael's birthday party. It was delicious.

2 It was very hot but you drank /didn't drink water after the race.

3 I ran /didn't run to school because I was late.

4 We went /didn't go to the funfair because it was raining. We stayed at home.

5 Paul and William did /didn't do their homework before going to the party. They didn't have time.

3 Answer the questions. Write numbers or dates as words.

1 Which is the tenth month of the year?   _October_

2 Which is the second day of the week?   _____

3 What date was last Monday?   _____

4 What's the last day of August?   _____

4 Write the questions in the Past simple. Then match the answers.

1 What time / you / get up yesterday?

   What time did you get up yesterday ?   [b]

2 you / find the necklace in the jewellery box?

   _____ ?   [ ]

3 the bride / wear a beautiful dress?

   _____ ?   [ ]

4 Where / you / lose your book?

   _____ ?   [ ]

5 Who / you / see at the funfair?

   _____ ?   [ ]

a In the science lab.

b At 8 am.

c My best friend.

d No, I didn't.

e Yes, she did.

Vocabulary and Grammar reference

Vocabulary

1 **Translate the words into your language. Add more words to the list.**

Celebrations		**Ordinal numbers**	
band	_____	first	_____
big wheel	_____	second	_____
bride	_____	third	_____
costume	_____	fourth	_____
funfair	_____	fifth	_____
groom	_____	ninth	_____
invitation	_____	twelfth	_____
party	_____	twentieth	_____
party hat	_____	twenty-first	_____
play party games	_____	thirtieth	_____
rollercoaster	_____	thirty-first	_____
wedding	_____		_____
_____		_____	_____
_____		_____	_____

Grammar

2 **Read and complete.**

did   go   eat   didn't   ~~wore~~

Past simple – Affirmative and negative

| I
He/She/It
We/You/They | [1] ___wore___ a cat costume | yesterday.
two days ago. |
| | didn't [2] _____ to school | last week. |

Past simple – Interrogative and short answers

Did		I he/she/it we/you/they	[3] _____ a piece of cake?
Yes,	_____		did.
No,	_____		[4] _____.
When	[5] _____		lose the ring?

Get ready for...

A1 Movers Reading and Writing Part 1

Think! **1** Look at the words in Activity 2. Complete the table.

People	Events	Things	Places
_____	_a wedding_	_____	_____
_____	_____	_____	_____
_____	_____	_____	_____

Do! **2** Look and read. Choose and write the correct words.

a wedding

a funfair

a party hat

a library

jewellery

a market

a band

a costume

1 Necklaces and rings are part of this. _____jewellery_____

2 A group of people who sing or play instruments. _____

3 You can buy fresh fruit and vegetables in this place. _____

4 You can ride a big wheel or rollercoaster there. _____

5 The bride and groom send you an invitation for this. _____

6 You can wear this on your head at a birthday party. _____

9 Holiday time!

Vocabulary

1 ⏱ **Look at Pupil's Book page 112 and write sentences about the picture.**

| sandcastle funfair ice cream snorkelling |

1 _____ *Lois is building a sandcastle.* _____
2 _____
3 _____
4 _____

2 **Look and match.**

1 bucket

2 build a sandcastle

3 beach towel

4 buy an ice cream

5 fishing net

6 sunhat

7 swimming trunks

8 rockpool

9 go surfing

10 swimsuit

11 go snorkelling

12 sunglasses

3 **Colour the words in Activity 2.**

◣ clothes ◣ place ◣ activities ◣ things

I'm learning

Sorting words using the same colour can help you remember vocabulary. Try with topics like parties (wedding parties, birthday parties ...), food (sweet, savoury ...) or clothes (summer, winter ...).

1 After you read **Read and complete. Then match.**

scissors　fishing net　bucket　help　quickly　well　dolphin

1 Lottie! Lois! Bo! Come _____quickly_____!
2 It's a dolphin! It's trapped in a _____!
3 I'm going to _____ you, little _____!
4 Bo, use the _____, not the _____!
5 _____ done, Bo!

a

b

c `1`

d

e

2 **Match the sentences.**

1 Bo and the children are
2 When Ash is snorkelling,
3 The dolphin is
4 The children can't get to the dolphin
5 Bo uses his scissors
6 The Discovery Team finds out

a he sees a dolphin.
b at the beach.
c to cut the fishing net.
d where the fishing net comes from.
e trapped in a fishing net.
f because it's very deep.

3 Values **Read and tick (✓). What values are there in this story? Give examples.**

work together　✓　appreciate animals　☐　work at school　☐

try new things　☐　be curious　☐　take turns　☐

share success　☐　take care of nature　☐

1 🎯 🎧 9.5 **Listen and match.** ⟫ Grammar reference, page 116

Claire | Paul | Zoe

Eve | Jim | Oliver

2 **Look and write.**

Sue → play football ✔
Mark and Chloe → go sailing ✗
Rob → go snorkelling ✗
Me → go climbing ✔
Martin and I → play tennis ✔
Sally → go fishing ✗

1 Sue is going to _____*play football*_____ .

2 Mark and Chloe aren't going _____
_____.

3 Rob isn't _____.

4 I _____.

5 Martin and I _____.

6 Sally _____.

3 **What are you going to do next week? Write.**

1 I'm going to _____ next week.

2 I'm not going to _____ next week.

Vocabulary and Grammar

1 **Complete the table.**

~~mountain biking~~   a bus tour   a theme park
a mountain   sightseeing   a waterpark   camping   hiking

go	take	visit	climb
mountain biking			

2 **Can you think of more words for the table in Activity 1?**

3 **Write the questions. Then answer.**

Mike's summer schedule

Monday	fly a kite in the park have dinner with my grandparents
Tuesday	climb a mountain with my friends
Wednesday	tidy up my room watch a film at home
Thursday	take a bus tour with my family
Friday	wash my parents' car go out with my friends
Saturday	visit a theme park
Sunday	go mountain biking with my family

1 when / Mike / take a bus tour?

When is Mike going to take a bus tour?
On Thursday.

2 he / tidy up his room on Wednesday?

3 he / climb a mountain with his family?

4 where / he / fly a kite?

5 what / he / do on Friday?

6 he / visit a theme park on Sunday?

Extra practice, page 115

CULTURE

1 **Complete the chart.**

Activities at the lake

Stay

Summer in Finland

swimming

Day trips

2 After you read **Read and answer.**

1 Where is Aleksi from?

He's from Finland.

2 When does Aleksi go to the cottage by the lake?

3 When does the sun go down in June and July?

4 What does Aleksi usually do at the lake?

5 What is Aleksi going to do this summer at the lake?

6 Where is Aleksi going to go on day trips this summer?

3 Draw a picture of one of the activities at the lake in Activity 1.

English in action
Making plans for summer

1 (9.14) **Listen and tick (✓). What are they going to do?**

1
a
b ✓

2
a
b

3
a
b

4
a
b

2 **Complete the dialogue.**

museum   let's   I'd like   ~~going~~   I'd prefer   I'd

What are we **(1)** _going_ to do this summer?

(2) _____ to go to the mountains.

(3) _____ to go to the beach.

OK, **(4)** _____ go to the beach.

What else are we going to do?

(5) _____ like to visit the toy museum in the city.

OK, let's go to the toy **(6)** _____!

It's going to be a great summer!

Pronunciation

3 (9.15) **Complete the table. Then listen and check.**

pink exciting boring bank sink wing thanks swimming drink

/ŋ/	/ŋk/
climbing	

Reading

1 After you read **Look at Pupil's Book page 120. Find the words in the text.**

1 an animal   *a dog*

2 you can put water or lemonade in this container _____

3 a country _____

4 a place with a lot of sand _____

5 a number bigger than 10 but smaller than 15 _____

2 **Correct the mistakes.**

1 Nergiz is <u>15</u> years old.

   Nergiz is 11 years old.

2 Nergiz walks her dog on the beach <u>every week</u>.

   _____

3 Nergiz found an old bottle on the <u>street</u>.

   _____

4 Nergiz wrote <u>an email</u> to Berat.

   _____

5 <u>Aslan</u> was the man who wrote the message.

   _____

3 💡 **Look. What's the message?**

a	b	c	d	e	f	g	h	i	j	k	l	m	n	o	p	q	r	s	t	u	v	w	x	y	z
★	●	♥	♣	★	●	♣	★	♣	♥	●	◆	♣	◆	♥	♥	◆	★	◆	◆	♣	◆	●	★	♥	●

♣ ♥   ◆ ★ ♣ ★   ♣ ◆   ♥ ★ ♣ ◆ .

My _____ .

♣   ★ ♣   ♣ ◆   ♥ ★ ★ ★   ◆ ★ ★ ★ ★ .

4 👥 **Write your own message and put it inside a bottle. You can reuse plastic bottles. Hide the bottles around school. Did any message get back to you?**

Writing

1 **Read and match.**

1 Dear   a from Alice

2 How   b Mum,

3 Love   c soon!

4 See you   d are you?

2 **Write a postcard to your friend.**

tip Writing

Look at the start (*Dear …*) and finish (*Love from …*) of the postcard. Use them in your postcard.

1 Plan

Read and answer. Make notes.

Who are you going to write to? _____ .

What's the weather like? _____ .

What did you do yesterday? _____ .

What are you going to do tomorrow? _____ .

Finish the postcard: _____ .

2 Write

Use your notes and write.

Dear _____ ,

_____ . The weather is _____ .

Yesterday I _____ .

Tomorrow I'm _____ .

See you soon! _____ .

3 Check your work ✔

Read your text again and tick (✓).

Correct start and finish? ☐   Correct spelling? ☐   Clear handwriting? ☐

3 **Write a postcard to a friend in class, at school or a relative who lives in a different town or city. Then draw a picture.**

1 **Look at Manuel's wish list and complete the text. Use the correct form of** *going to* **and the words from the box.**

visit   go   ~~eat~~   climb   tidy up   build

I want to: ✓   I don't want to: ✗

1 ✗
2 ✓
3 ✗
4 ✓
5 ✗
6 ✓

My summer wish list

This is my wish list for this summer. First, I'm
(1) ___not going to eat___ a lot of ice cream.
Second, I'm **(2)**_____
camping with my family. I love campsites! Third,
I'm **(3)**_____ a mountain because
I'm scared! Fourth, I'm **(4)**_____
a sandcastle with my sister. She's going to be very
happy with me! Fifth, I **(5)**_____
a water park. It's so boring! And sixth, I
(6)_____ my room. I don't like it
but I know that my parents are going to be happy.

2 **Create your own wish list for this summer. Then write.**

This is my wish list for this summer.

First, I _____.

Second, _____.

Third, _____.

Fourth, _____.

Fifth, _____.

And sixth, _____.

Self-evaluation

My work in Unit 9 is OK / good / excellent.

My favourite lesson is the one about _____.

I can _____.

I need to work more on _____.

1 Order the words to make sentences.

1 not   buy   I'm   to   an ice cream   going   .

_____ *I'm not going to buy an ice cream.* _____

2 are   to   some lemonade   they   drink   going   .

_____

3 a new   my sister   going   beach towel   to   is   buy   .

_____

4 isn't   play baseball   going   this weekend   she   to   .

_____

5 to   you   in the band   going   aren't   this weekend   play   .

_____

2 Find and circle the words. Write.

I	A	M	R	U	O	T	S	U	B	G
C	L	I	M	B	O	I	N	G	H	T
O	V	C	A	M	P	I	N	G	I	I
S	I	T	A	T	H	E	M	E	K	P
G	N	I	E	E	S	T	H	G	I	S
W	A	T	E	R	P	A	R	K	N	A
R	K	T	H	I	S	S	U	M	G	M
E	R	W	I	T	H	M	Y	M	U	M

1 visit a   ____*waterpark*____

2 go _____

3 go _____

4 go _____

5 _____ a mountain

6 take a _____

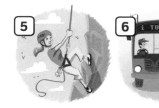

3 🔍 **Look at the letters which aren't circled in Activity 2. Can you find a message?**

The hidden message is:

_I_ _____

_____

4 Complete the questions and answers.

1 Are you _____ to take photos of the countryside? Yes, I _____ .

2 _____ your brother going to wash our car? No, he _____ .

3 _____ are you going to visit the new theme park? We're _____ to visit it today.

4 _____ Sally and Amelia going to see the concert? _____ , they are.

5 Are you and Paul _____ to go to the funfair this weekend? No, we _____ .

Vocabulary and Grammar reference

Vocabulary

1 **Translate the words into your language. Add more words to the list.**

Holidays on the beach

beach towel _____

bucket _____

build a castle _____

buy an ice cream _____

fishing net _____

go snorkelling _____

go surfing _____

rockpool _____

sunglasses _____

sunhat _____

swimming trunks _____

swimsuit _____

_____ _____

_____ _____

_____ _____

Holidays in the city

go sightseeing _____

take a bus tour _____

visit a theme park _____

visit a waterpark _____

_____ _____

_____ _____

_____ _____

Holidays outside the city

climb a mountain _____

go camping _____

go hiking _____

go mountain biking _____

_____ _____

_____ _____

Grammar

2 **Read and complete.**

aren't   to   ~~'s~~   Am   When   are   going   go   visit   she   'm not

be going to – Affirmative

I	'm going to	
He/She/It	¹ __'s__ going to	go climbing.
We/You/They	're going ² ____	

be going to – Negative

I	'm not ³ _____ to	
He/She/It	isn't going to	⁵ _____ surfing.
We/You/They	⁴ _____ going to	

be going to – Interrogative and short answers

⁶ _____	I	going to take a bus tour?
Is	he/ ⁷ _____ /it	
Are	we/you/they	

Yes, I am. Yes, he/she/it is. Yes, we/you/they ⁸ _____	No, I ⁹ _____. No, he/she/it isn't. No, we/you/they aren't.

¹⁰ _____	am	I	going to ¹¹ _____ a waterpark?
	is	he/she/it	
	are	we/you/they	

Get ready for...

A1 Movers Reading and Writing Part 5

Do! **1** 🎯 **Look at the pictures and read the story. Write 1, 2 or 3 words to complete the sentences.**

Family holidays

Last summer, Bob and his family went camping near the beach for their holiday.
'I'm going to go surfing first, and then I'm going to build a very big sandcastle!' Bob said.
'Oh … I'm going to help you with the sandcastle, Bob!' Bob's sister said.
Bob's family arrived at the campsite. They put up the tent and got ready to go to the beach: sunglasses, sunhats and beach towels.
'Oh, no!' Bob's dad said looking at the black clouds in the sky. 'The weather is changing! I think it's going to rain!'
And it started to rain heavily.

1 Bob and his family were at a campsite near _____ *the beach* _____ .

2 Bob and his sister wanted to _____ together.

3 They didn't go to the beach because _____ was cold and rainy.

Bob's family was now inside the car. They looked a bit sad.
'What are we going to do now?' Bob asked.
'I know!' Bob's mum said. 'Why don't we take a bus tour around town?'
'Yes!' Bob's dad said. 'And then we can have some burgers for dinner, too!'
And Bob's family went to town and had the best day of their holiday together.

4 Bob's family took _____ around town.

5 Bob's family had _____ for dinner.

6 That was the best day they _____ that holiday.

Language booster 3

1 **Complete the words. Then number the pictures.**

1 g<u>e</u>t dr<u>e</u>ss<u>e</u>d
2 g_t __dressed
3 p_t _n
4 t_k e _ff
5 l_s_
6 inv_t_

a

b

c [1]

d

e

f

2 **Read and circle.**

1 I get dressed / get undressed in the morning.

2 I don't want to put on / lose my favourite toy.

3 I take off / invite my coat in the house.

4 I always lose / invite my friends to my birthday party.

5 I get dressed / get undressed before I have a shower.

6 I put on / take off my pyjamas when I go to bed.

3 **Complete the sentences for you.**

1 In the morning, I get _____ at _____ o'clock.

2 I put on my _____.

3 In the evening, I get _____ at _____ o'clock.

4 I take off my _____.

5 I don't want to lose my _____.

6 I want to invite _____ to _____.

4 **Look at the pictures. Match them to the sentences.**

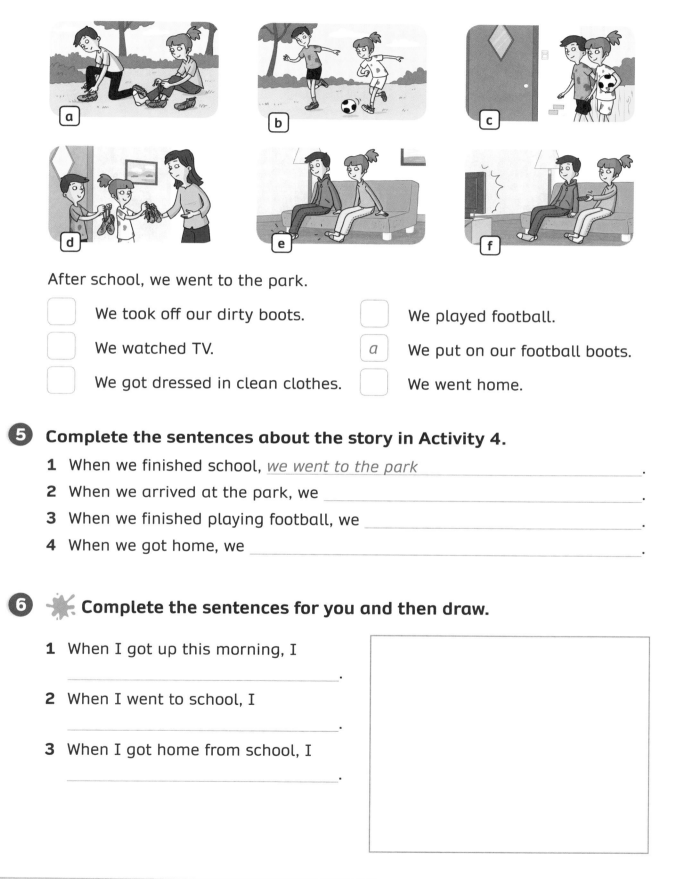

After school, we went to the park.

☐ We took off our dirty boots.

☐ We watched TV.

☐ We got dressed in clean clothes.

☐ We played football.

a We put on our football boots.

☐ We went home.

5 **Complete the sentences about the story in Activity 4.**

1 When we finished school, *we went to the park* _____.

2 When we arrived at the park, we _____.

3 When we finished playing football, we _____.

4 When we got home, we _____.

6 **Complete the sentences for you and then draw.**

1 When I got up this morning, I

_____.

2 When I went to school, I

_____.

3 When I got home from school, I

_____.

New Year

1 **Find and circle the words. Write.**

1

New Year's _____Eve_____

2

New Year's _____

3

_____

4

_____

5

New Year's _____

2 **Find the hidden message in Activity 1.**

The hidden message is: _I_ _____

_____

3 **Write your New Year's resolutions.**

World Friendship Day

1 Complete the puzzle. Find the secret word.

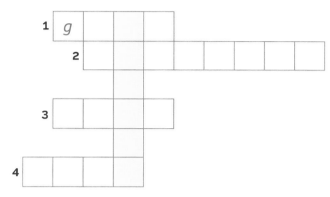

On World Friendship Day,

1 we give a small …

2 we can make a friendship …

3 we write a message or a …

4 we make a …

2 Draw a picture. Write a poem for World Friendship Day.

World Book Day

1 Order the letters and write. Then match.

a

b

c

1 c s h r a e r t a c
c_haracters_

2 e p d a r a
p _ _ _ _ _

3 y b e s l m s a
a _ _ _ _ _ _ _

2 Remember Pupil's Book page 130. Write the names of the characters in Emily's text. Can you think of more examples?

_____

_____

_____

3 Draw the cover of your favourite book. Why do you like it?

I like this book because _____

_____

_____

_____

_____

_____

4 Present your book cover to the class.

Communication activities

Unit ① Student A

Ask Student B about: • Music   • Maths   • Natural Science

	Monday	Tuesday	Wednesday	Thursday	Friday
9:00		Social Science			English
11:00			English	ICT	
1:30	English	PE	Social Science	Art	ICT

When do we have Music?

We have Music on … at …

Unit ② Student A

What's in the kitchen? Ask and answer to find out.

cereal	fruit	coffee	eggs	milk	water	lemonade	vegetables
✗			✗		✓ a bottle	✓ 2 cans	

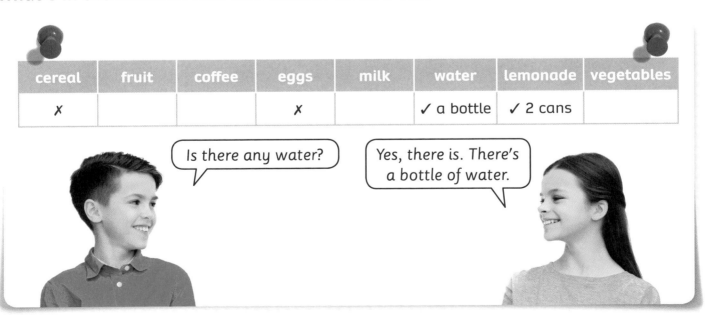

Is there any water?

Yes, there is. There's a bottle of water.

Communication activities

Unit  3

Think and number 1 (the most), 2 or 3 (the least). Then ask and answer.

boring		dangerous		delicious		famous	
	tennis		climbing		cupcake		Taylor Swift
	baseball		canoeing		crisps		Justin Bieber
	football		skating		sandwich		Selena Gómez

I think football is more boring than tennis, but baseball is the most boring. Do you agree?

No. I think baseball is more boring than tennis, but football is the most boring.

Unit 4

Ask and answer to find the differences.

What are the waiters doing?

In my picture they're serving food.

In my picture they're serving drinks.

Ask and answer to find out what Mindy and Micky can do.

1 Complete the sentences about Mindy. Use three different adverbs.
2 Ask Student B what Micky can do and write.
3 Answer Student B's questions about Mindy.

About Mindy!

a Mindy _____ .

b She _____ .

c She _____ .

About Micky!

a Micky can sing _____ .

b He can play computer games

_____ .

c He can dance _____ .

> Can Micky sing loudly?

> No, he can't. He can sing slowly.

Ask and answer to find out where Ethan and Ahmed were.
Then answer the questions.

- When were they in the same place at the same time?
- When weren't they in the same place at the same time?

	yesterday	three days ago	last Saturday
10 o'clock	clothes shop		train station
3 o'clock		car park	park
7 o'clock	theatre		

Ethan

	yesterday	three days ago	last Saturday
10 o'clock		bus stop	
3 o'clock		Granny's house	park
7 o'clock	theatre		

Ahmed

> Where was Ethan at 3 o'clock yesterday?

> He was at the zoo.

Communication activities

Unit

What did Tommy do last week? Ask and answer to find out.

play football   watch TV   use clay to make a jug   need to buy some new shoes

Monday	Tuesday	Wednesday	Thursday	Friday	Saturday	Sunday
He arrived late at school. He started piano lessons.					He went to his cousins' house.	He visited a museum.

When did Tommy play football?

He played football on Wednesday.

Unit

You and your friend had a busy week last week! Ask and answer. Did you do the same thing on the same day?

run to school   go to a funfair   see a film   go to a party
have dinner at a restaurant   go to a wedding

	20th May	21st May	22nd May	23rd May	24th May	25th May
Your week						
Your friend's week						

When did you run to school?

I ran to school on 24th May!

Unit

Kayla and Robbie are going on holiday to the USA. They aren't going together, but they want to meet when they're there. Ask and answer to find out what they are going to do each day of their holiday. When are they going to do the same thing?

	Monday	Tuesday	Wednesday	Thursday	Friday	Saturday
Robbie	go fishing			go to the beach	visit a theme park	
Kayla		go surfing	go hiking			go sightseeing

> What's Kayla going to do on Monday?

> She's going to take a bus tour.

Unit 1

Ask Student A about: • Social Science • Art • ICT • PE

	Monday	Tuesday	Wednesday	Thursday	Friday
9:00	Maths		Maths	Natural Science	English
11:00	Music	Natural Science	English		Maths
1:30	English				

> When do we have Social Science?

> We have Social Science on ... at ...

Communication activities

What's in the kitchen? Ask and answer to find out.

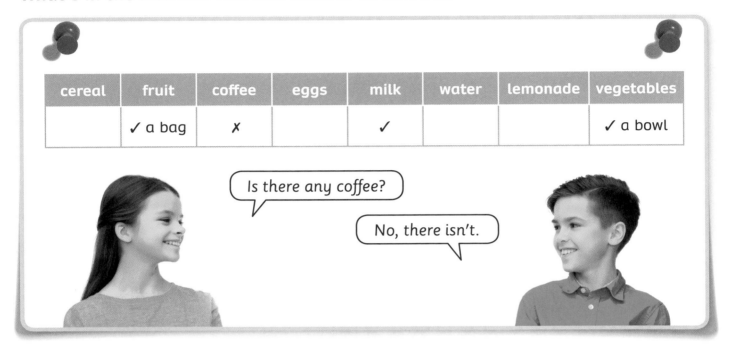

cereal	fruit	coffee	eggs	milk	water	lemonade	vegetables
	✓ a bag	✗		✓			✓ a bowl

Is there any coffee?

No, there isn't.

Think and number 1 (the most), 2 or 3 (the least). Then ask and answer.

boring		dangerous		delicious		famous	
tennis		climbing		cupcake		Taylor Swift	
baseball		canoeing		crisps		Justin Bieber	
football		skating		sandwich		Selena Gómez	

I think football is more boring than tennis, but baseball is the most boring. Do you agree?

No. I think baseball is more boring than tennis, but football is the most boring.

Ask and answer to find the differences.

> What are the waiters doing?

> In my picture they're serving food.

> In my picture they're serving drinks.

Unit 5

Ask and answer to find out what Mindy and Micky can do.

1 Complete the sentences about Micky. Use three different adverbs.
2 Ask Student A what Mindy can do and write.
3 Answer Student A's questions about Micky.

All about Micky!

a Micky _____ .
b He _____ .
c He _____ .

All about Mindy!

a Mindy can sew _____ .
b She can build _____ .
c She can climb trees _____ .

> Can Mindy sew well?

> Yes, she can.

Communication activities

Ask and answer to find out where Ethan and Ahmed were. Then answer the questions.

- When were they in the same place at the same time?
- When weren't they in the same place at the same time?

Ethan

	yesterday	three days ago	last Saturday
10 o'clock		library	
3 o'clock	zoo		
7 o'clock		train station	café

Ahmed

	yesterday	three days ago	last Saturday
10 o'clock	car park		football practice
3 o'clock	zoo		park
7 o'clock		bus stop	café

> Where was Ahmed at 3 o'clock three days ago?

> He was at Granny's house.

What did Tommy do last week? Ask and answer to find out.

arrive late at school   visit a museum   start piano lessons   go to his cousins' house

Monday	Tuesday	Wednesday	Thursday	Friday	Saturday	Sunday
	He watched TV.	He played football.	He used clay to make a jug.	He needed to buy some new shoes.		

> When did Tommy arrive late at school?

> He arrived late at school on Monday.

You and your friend had a busy week last week! Ask and answer. Did you do the same thing on the same day?

> have dinner at a restaurant   run to school   see a film
> go to a funfair   go to a party   go to a wedding

	20th May	21st May	22nd May	23rd May	24th May	25th May
Your week						
Your friend's week						

When did you have dinner at a restaurant?

I had dinner at a restaurant on 20th May!

Kayla and Robbie are going on holiday to the USA. They aren't going together, but they want to meet when they're there. Ask and answer to find out what they are going to do each day of their holiday. When are they going to do the same thing?

	Monday	Tuesday	Wednesday	Thursday	Friday	Saturday
Robbie		go sightseeing	go mountain biking			go to the beach
Kayla	take a bus tour			visit a waterpark	visit a theme park	

What's Robbie going to do on Monday?

He's going to go fishing.

Say it!

Unit 1

Do you want to play football tomorrow morning?

Sorry, I can't. / I'm not free.

What about Sunday?

Let's meet at four in the park.

Unit 2

Can I help you?

Can I have six apples / some grapes, please?

Here you are! Anything else?

No, that's it, thanks!

That's five pounds, please.

Unit 3

Excuse me, can you tell me the way to the park, please?

Turn right at the supermarket.

Turn left at the hospital.

Go straight ahead.

Go across the road.

It's on the left.

Unit 4

I need an ambulance, please.

My address is …

My phone number is …

He's got a broken leg.

Unit 5

What shall we do?

Do you want to play a computer game?

Not really. I'd rather play chess.

Unit 6

I was at the clothes shop.

What was it like?

It was very busy.

How was it?

You should go and see it!

Unit 7

What should I do?

You should wear old clothes.

Should I work quickly?

No, you shouldn't!

Unit 8

What's the matter?

I can't find my book.

When did you last see it?

I had it when I went to school.

Let's go and look there.

Unit 9

I'd like to go to the beach!

I'd prefer to swim in the pool.

Let's go to the waterpark!

Progress path

Read and write. Then tick (✓) .

Unit 2

Is there a bowl / cup of tea?
Yes, there is / are.

Unit 1

When does Lottie have Maths?

Monday		
9–10	Maths	She
10–11	break	
11–12	Natural Science	_____
12–1	lunch	
1–2	PE	
2–2.30	break	
2.30–3.30	English	_____
4.30	swimming lesson	

Unit 3

What is it?

l a l f r a w e t

It's a

_ _ _ _ _ _ _ _ _ _ .

Starter Unit

twenty-two +
sixty-three =
eighty-five

2__ + ___ = ___

Unit 4

You must / mustn't
be late for class.